"Knohl not only documents a series of transformations in Israelite messianism but also meticulously discusses their political ramifications. This thought-provoking work is a must-read for anyone interested in the biblical world as well as in Jewish thought and politics throughout history."

—ISHAY ROSEN-ZVI, chair of the Department of
Jewish Philosophy and Talmud, Tel Aviv University

"*The Messiah Confrontation* is the product of meticulous research, yet takes away one's breath. It can be seen as a key that allows us to understand messianic phenomena hundreds of years after the writing of biblical literature, and in reality until this very day. Knohl lays the foundation for the development of a narrative that allows us to classify, categorize, and evaluate key events throughout Jewish history in light of messianic tension. In essence, it provokes the reader and the scholar to develop a new narrative of Jewish history—one based entirely on the tensions between different messianic ideas."

—DOV SCHWARTZ, professor of Jewish
philosophy, Bar Ilan University

"In *The Messiah Confrontation*, Israel Knohl, one of the leading Bible scholars of our time, proposes an original and provocative history of messianism from the Bible through ancient Judaism, culminating in a new interpretation of the trial and death of Jesus. This profoundly learned and accessibly written book will be of great interest to scholars and laypersons alike, and especially to all readers concerned with the fraught history of Judaism and Christianity and their many intersections."

—DAVID STERN, Harry Starr Professor of
Classical and Modern Hebrew and Jewish
Literature, Harvard University

The Messiah Confrontation

The Messiah

University of Nebraska Press

LINCOLN

Confrontation

Pharisees versus Sadducees and the Death of Jesus

ISRAEL KNOHL

Translated by David Maisel

The Jewish Publication Society
PHILADELPHIA

Library of Congress Control Number: 2022008578

Set in ITC Galliard Pro by Mikala R. Kolander.

Contents

Acknowledgments

The original Hebrew version of this work was based mostly on words I spoke to Omri Shasha, a PhD candidate, which he recorded and edited. I would like to thank him for his skillful work.

Later, the book enjoyed the wisdom of my two editors at the Kinneret–Zmora-Bitan publishing house, which published the Hebrew version: Yael Naamani and Samuel Rozner.

David Maisel, my gifted translator for more than twenty years, prepared the English translation.

Joy Weinberg, managing editor of The Jewish Publication Society, adapted and edited the work very skillfully, substantively updating it with new material for an English-speaking audience. My copyeditor, Amy Pattullo, helped to clarify significant issues.

Finally, I would like to thank The Jewish Publication Society and its director, Rabbi Barry Schwartz, and the University of Nebraska Press for copublishing this work

Introduction

A few years ago, on the Jewish New Year, I walked from my home in the German Colony in Jerusalem to the Western Wall in the Old City. When I arrived, the Temple Wall enclosure was full of people from end to end. Among the worshipers, a large group of men and young people stood out. They were all dressed in white and wore white headdresses.

Their prayer leader, who had a silvery beard, stood right next to the Wall. Suddenly he raised his head, and loudly and with great emotion cried:

"The king that sits on a lofty throne."

Two sturdy young men to the left and right of the prayer leader took a large picture out of a linen bag. In the center of the picture was an old Hasidic leader who had passed away several years earlier. He had a long beard and his arms were raised. Between his arms the following words appeared:

"I am the king!"

The two young men lifted up the picture and placed it against the stones of the Wall, and the prayer leader intoned in a tremolo:

"The king that sits on a lofty throne."

In the tradition of the sages rooted in the Bible, the New Year is the day when God is crowned King of the Universe, and the shofar (ram's horn) is blown in honor of his coronation. This is expressed in Psalm 47, which is read seven times before the shofar is sounded:

God has gone up with a shout, the Lord
   with the sound of a trumpet.

Sing praises to God, sing praises! Sing
  praises to our King, sing praises!
For God is the king of all the earth;
  sing praises with a psalm!
God reigns over the nations; God sits on
  his holy throne. (Ps. 47:5–8)

The scene I witnessed by the Western Wall on the New Year was
a contemporary reflection of the view, held by a number of scholars,
that on the New Year not only is God again crowned king of all
the nations, but the king of the house of David is again crowned
king of Zion and Judah on this day in the Temple in Jerusalem.

The group by the Wall consisted of followers of Rabbi Yisroel Ber
Odesser. This rabbi, who in his youth lived in Tiberias and Safed,
became known for a mysterious note that he found. His followers
believe that Rabbi Nachman of Breslov, a renowned Hasidic leader
whose grave in the Ukraine is visited by tens of thousands of Breslov
Hasidim every New Year, sent this note specifically to Rabbi Yisroel
Ber Odesser, who was born in 1888, seventy-eight years after Rabbi
Nachman died. Rabbi Odesser's followers call him "the master of
the note." Unlike the other Breslov Hasidim, who go to Uman in
the Ukraine on the New Year, the followers of the master of the
note stay in Jerusalem and perform the ceremony I saw.

The ceremony combined two acts of coronation: the coronation
of God, described as "the king who sits on a lofty throne," and
the coronation of the messianic leader, the master of the note,
whom Rabbi Odesser's followers regard as the incarnation of Rabbi
Nachman of Breslov and the king-Messiah.

Near the group of followers of the master of the note stood
another group. The prayer leader of this group was a kabbalist
with red hair dressed in tattered clothes. He read the words of
the prayers with great emotion, loudly and while weeping. It was
obvious that the other group displeased him. They, for their part,
muttered criticisms of him and called him "the old serpent."

The kabbalist dressed in tattered clothes probably saw himself as an incarnation of the "suffering servant" of Isaiah 52–53, a poor and despised figure who atones for the sins of his people. To the kabbalist and his followers, the messianic arguments of the master of the note and his followers were fallacious and unacceptable. The kabbalist's followers do not claim that their leader is a Messiah; they expect the Messiah to come in the future. Yet to the master of the note and his followers, their opponent, the kabbalist, is an incarnation of the evil serpent who seduced Eve in the Garden of Eden; he is a hypocrite, spouting fake tears.

The scene I witnessed by the Western Wall on that New Year's Day was a contemporary manifestation of the vitality of the messianic idea in the Jewish world of our time—and of the controversies that this idea has given rise to from its beginnings until now.

This book traces the appearances of the messianic idea from the prophet Isaiah to the Bar Kokhba revolt. It demonstrates the dramatic, many-sided, and fascinating controversy about the messianic idea within the Bible itself.

Two main tendencies are to be found in the books of the Bible. On the one hand, the Torah, and especially its priestly part, seeks to elevate God and create a clear distinction between the human and the Divine. According to this view, God has nothing to do with human biological processes such as birth, marriage, and dying. The human life cycle distinguishes God—who is not born, does not marry, has no progeny, and has a deathless existence—from mortal humanity. An unbridgeable gulf separates the human and the Divine.

On the other hand, some of the books of the prophets and some of the psalms approach this idea very differently. These texts seek to elevate the image of a king, either the present one sitting on the throne or a future, hoped-for king who is sometimes called a Messiah. This king-Messiah is given divine characteristics. He is called the "son of God," is described as sitting beside God in heaven, and is sometimes even given the name of God: "the Mighty God" or "God our righteousness."

As we follow the course of the two streams, the ways in which they developed and their points of convergence and disagreement, we come upon a basin into which these two streams flowed: the trial of Jesus of Nazareth before the High Priest in Jerusalem. This of course was a dramatic and fateful moment in the history of the Jewish people, and in fact in the history of the whole of Western culture.

Jesus's trial was ultimately a dramatic encounter of these two biblical ideological approaches. While Jesus in his actions and message represented the position of the prophets and the psalms, which expected the arrival of a godlike Messiah, the judges who condemned him to death held the antimessianic position, which ruled out the possibility of a Messiah. Meanwhile, the great majority of the people of Israel generally agreed with Jesus on this position. The people were aligned with the Jewish sect known as the Pharisees, who believed in a godlike warrior Messiah who would rescue the Jews from Roman rule.

Unfortunately, Jesus's judges were not Pharisees, the predecessors of the rabbinic sages. Jesus's judges were Sadducees, engaged in a bitter controversy with the Pharisees on this very question of the Messiah. In other words, the trial of Jesus was not a confrontation of Jewish and Christian doctrines, but a conflict between two internal Jewish positions in which Jesus and the Pharisees were on the same side.

The scene I witnessed at the Western Wall was a marvelous illustration of the fact that the messianic idea of both Jesus and the Pharisees—a king-Messiah of divine status—is still alive today.

This analysis has far-reaching consequences for the relationship between Jews and Christians. It demonstrates that the idea that the "Jewish people" killed Jesus is fundamentally mistaken. First, the Romans killed Jesus (Jews were not allowed to perform executions when they lived under Roman rule). Second, although the great majority of the Jewish people did not accept Jesus as the Messiah, most Jews had a conception of a Messiah similar to that of Jesus.

On October 28, 1965, the second Vatican Ecumenical Council in Rome took the very positive step of declaring that the Jewish people as a whole should not be blamed for the death of Jesus. Important as this declaration was, it was not based on a detailed study of the historical events. By casting new light on the historical events surrounding Jesus's crucifixion, this book offers the first-ever detailed historical basis for that declaration.

I hope that *The Messiah Confrontation* will give rise to a new discourse between Jews and Christians and help to heal this vital relationship.

The Messiah Confrontation

Birth of the Messianic Figure

An ancient legend in the Jerusalem Talmud relates that a Jew was plowing his field with his ox, and the ox bellowed loudly.[1] An Arab passer-by said to him: "Jew, Jew, loosen your ox and release your plow, for your Temple has just been destroyed." A few moments later the ox bellowed again, and the Arab said to him, "Jew, harness your ox and your plow, and return to plowing the field, for the Messiah has just been born."

This fine legend, which relates that the Messiah was born on the very day and at the very hour when the Temple was destroyed, is a suitable starting point for understanding the emergence of the messianic idea in Judaism, for the idea has its beginnings in a series of events that led to the destruction of the kingdoms of Israel and Judah. Once this core idea of a Jewish Messiah took root, it would take different forms in various periods throughout Jewish history, up through our present day. Put succinctly, Jewish messianism has had critical influence on Jewish and general history—and, as we will see in this book especially, on the death of Jesus.

As for its first appearance in the Hebrew Bible, I am referring specifically to the meeting between the prophet Isaiah, son of Amoz, and Ahaz, King of Judah, which took place in 733 BCE and is described in chapter 7 of the book of Isaiah. The chapter tells of a Syrian-Israelite coalition in which Rezin, the king of Syria, joined Pekah, son of Remaliah, the king of Israel, to fight against Judah and capture Jerusalem: "Let us go up against Judah and terrify it, and let us conquer it for ourselves, and set up the son of Tabeel as king in the midst of it" (7:6). They plotted to breach the walls of Jerusalem, depose Ahaz the king of Judah, and end the house of David's more than 250-year rule in Jerusalem. A person named "son of Tabeel" would replace Ahaz and be subservient to them.

Scholars differ over the reason for this confrontation. Some claim it was a land dispute concerning control of the territories beyond the River Jordan. Others see it in connection with a broader development: the rise of the superpower of that period, the kingdom of Assyria. In those years, Tiglath-pileser III, king of Assyria, set out on a campaign of conquest, subjugating numerous territories in the Middle East (with the help of improved weapons of war and siege implements, among other factors) and making Assyria into an imperial power. Some scholars think that the kings of Israel and Syria were trying to forge a local alliance against Assyria, and wanted Ahaz, the king of Judah, to join them. When he refused, Syria and Israel decided to conquer Judah and force it to join their coalition.

Whatever the case, there was great fear in Jerusalem and in the heart of its king, of which the prophet Isaiah gave a vivid description: "His heart and the heart of his people shook as the trees of the forest shake before the wind" (Isa. 7:2). Then, Isaiah relates, God sent him to Ahaz to deliver a message:

> Go forth to meet Ahaz, you and Shearjashub your son, at the end of the conduit of the upper pool on the highway to the Fuller's Field, and say to him, "Take heed, be quiet, do not fear, and do not let your heart be faint because of these two smoldering stumps of firebrands, at the fierce anger of Rezin and Syria and the son of Remaliah." (7:3–4)

The kings gathered against Ahaz were "smoldering stumps of firebrands": embers about to be extinguished, kings without power. They were nothing to be afraid of.

About ten years ago I joined the late archaeologist David Amit at an excavation he directed in the center of Jerusalem, close to the present-day Independence Park and Cats' Square. As part of a plan to build a new museum in the area, the Antiquities Authority had asked for an excavation to be carried out on site, and there Amit found the remains of a dam and, next to it, a water channel. The findings were dated to the second half of the eighth century BCE, and it seems the dam functioned to collect the water and convey it to ancient Jerusalem, in the area of the City of David. Amit suggested that this was the "conduit of the upper pool" where the dramatic meeting between Isaiah and Ahaz took place. Indeed, the area excavated by Amit was full of currents of water, and the whole place was filled with mud as a result of the winter rains.

One can imagine King Ahaz going up to the conduit of the upper pool to examine the water installations and prepare for war and a siege, and there meeting the prophet Isaiah, who conveyed a reassuring message: "Thus says the Lord God: It shall not stand, and it shall not come to pass" (Isa. 7:7). Ahaz had to believe and trust in God, for nothing bad was going to happen.

In order to increase his sense of security, the prophet suggested in the name of God that the king ask God for a sign that this would indeed be the case: "Ask a sign of the Lord your God; let it be deep as Sheol or high as heaven" (Isa. 7:11). But Ahaz, in a kind of demonstration of piety, declined the invitation: "I will not ask, and I will not put the Lord to the test" (7:12). The prophet reacted angrily: "Hear then, O house of David! Is it too little for you to weary men, that you weary my God also?" (Isa. 7:13). Then, against Ahaz's will, Isaiah reports, God gave the king a mysterious sign:

> Therefore the Lord himself will give you a sign. Behold a young woman shall conceive and bear a son, and he shall call his name Immanuel. (7:14)

Why was God angry? It seems that behind Ahaz's declaration that he did not want to put God to the test stood doubt and lack of faith. A passage in the book of Kings fills out the picture, explaining to us what Ahaz was actually doing at that time. Ahaz turned to the king of Assyria, sent him silver and gold from the Temple and the royal treasury, and asked him to save him: "So Ahaz sent messengers to Tiglath-pileser king of Assyria, saying, 'I am your servant and your son. Come up, and rescue me from the hand of the king of Syria and from the hand of the king of Israel, who are attacking me'" (2 Kings 16:7). Ahaz did not trust Isaiah's promise, and on political grounds he simply preferred to depend on the ascending power in the area, the Assyrian empire.

God, meanwhile, viewed Ahaz's act of turning to a foreign power as lack of trust in God. This appears to be the meaning of the sign God sends: the birth of son to a young woman. Although scholars dispute some of the particulars concerning that son—was he the son of a princess of the royal house or a son of the prophet?—it is clear that the real sign was to be found in the name of the child: Immanuel (God is with us). God was asking Ahaz to trust in him instead of depending on Assyrian military and political power.

From the historical point of view, this was a decisive moment in the history of the kingdom of Judah. The king of Judah described himself as the servant of the king of Assyria: an extraordinary statement representing a political move of great significance. At this moment, Ahaz was renouncing Judah's independence and making himself into a kind of vassal of Tiglath-pileser III. From this time onward, except for a short interval, Judah would not exist as an independent state. The independence that King David had gained in Jerusalem more than two hundred years earlier ceased to exist. In a certain sense, this moment anticipated the physical destruction of Jerusalem only a few generations later.

Moreover, this moment not only contained the seeds of the fall of the kingdom of Judah, but was also the beginning of the fall of the kingdom of Israel. Tiglath-pileser III responded to Ahaz's request and came to the area. He conquered and brought the kingdom of Syria to an end that same year, and at the same

BIRTH OF THE MESSIANIC FIGURE 5

time he conquered large parts of the kingdom of Israel in the coastal regions, the Galilee, and beyond the River Jordan. And it was then and there, as Tiglath-pileser made those regions into Assyrian provinces, that the process of exiling the ten tribes began. The kingdom of Israel shrank dramatically, and within ten years Assyria conquered Israel's capital, Samaria—an act that led to the final destruction of the kingdom of Israel and the disappearance of the ten tribes into the Assyrian melting pot.

In many respects, the year 733 BCE marked the beginning of the end of Judah and Israel. Isaiah was of course aware of the drama taking place in the Northern Kingdom, and in the following chapter the prophet described the depression and distress that prevailed there:

> They will look to the earth, but behold, distress and darkness, the gloom of anguish; and they will be thrust into thick darkness. But there will be no gloom for her that was in anguish. In the former time, he brought into contempt the land of Zebulun and the land of Naphtali, but in the latter time he will make glorious the way of the sea, the land beyond the Jordan, Galilee of the nations. (Isa. 8:22–9:1)

The anguish, distress, and darkness were due to the Assyrian king's conquest of the lands of Zebulun and Naphtali. The end of these verses seems to describe the exiling of the inhabitants of those areas and the creation of the three aforementioned new Assyrian provinces: in the coastal region, beyond the Jordan, and in the Galilee.

The Assyrian system of conquest included exiling the local inhabitants, dispersing them throughout the Assyrian empire, and resettling in the conquered territories people exiled from other provinces. In this way, the Assyrian regime effaced the local national identities. Thus the conquered areas of the kingdom of Israel ceased to be Israelite, and the same happened very soon afterwards to Israel's capital, Samaria. Isaiah, who saw Judah and

Israel as a single entity belonging to a single people, lamented the situation in the kingdom of Israel.

But suddenly, within his description of the distress and darkness that prevailed there, the prophet had a vision of a great light: "The people who walked in darkness have seen a great light; those who dwelt in a land of deep darkness, on them has light shined. Thou hast multiplied the nation, thou hast increased its joy; they rejoice before thee as with joy at the harvest, as men rejoice when they divide the spoil" (Isa. 9:2–3). The rod, which for Isaiah symbolized Assyrian rule, was about to be broken, as happened in Israel's sudden deliverance from Midian in the time of Gideon: "For the yoke of his burden, and the staff of his shoulder, the rod of his oppressor, thou hast broken as on the day of Midian" (9:4).[2]

Isaiah gives a bold description of that future day of salvation: "For every boot of the tramping warrior in battle tumult and every garment rolled in blood will be burned for fuel for the fire" (Isa. 9:5). These are the abandoned boots and the blood-soaked garments of Assyrian soldiers. Isaiah pictures a future victory over Assyria in which the garments and boots of the enemy are burned after their defeat. And lo and behold! Appearing after the defeat is a wondrous and mysterious figure who is all-important for our study:

> For to us a child is born, to us a child is given; and the government will be upon his shoulder, and his name will be called "Wonderful Counselor, Mighty God, Everlasting Father, Prince of Peace."
>
> Of the increase of his government and of peace there will be no end, upon the throne of David and over his kingdom, to establish it and to uphold it with justice and truth and with righteousness from this time forth and for evermore.
>
> The zeal of the Lord of hosts will do this. (9:6–7)

What is the prophet describing here? Who is the child who is to be born? What is the meaning of these four very special titles:

"Wonderful Counselor, Mighty God, Everlasting Father, Prince of Peace"?

Whose coronation was it? One of the suggestions made by scholars is that the mysterious child was none other than Hezekiah the son of Ahaz, the king who would inherit the throne after the death of his father.[3] The title "Mighty God" hints at the king's name, Hezekiah, which means "God is my strength." This interpretation is supported by, among other things, the year in which the prophecy was made: 727 BCE, an especially dramatic year from a political point of view. In that year, six years after the meeting at the conduit of the upper pool, Ahaz the king of Judah died, as did the king and founder of the Assyrian empire, Tiglath-pileser III. According to this view, with the ostensible abatement of the Assyrian threat, Isaiah was said to have been filled with political and historical optimism and made joyful predictions about the new king who would sit on the throne of the kingdom of Judah.

But this reading of the verses raises serious problems. First of all, the prophecy says nothing about the consecration of a new king, but speaks of the birth of a child: "For to us a child is born, to us a child is given." Second, it is hard to believe that Isaiah's political mood was improved by the Assyrian king's death in that year, for in that very year Isaiah made another prophecy that expresses precisely the opposite position:

> Rejoice not, O Philistia, all of you, that the rod which smote you is broken, for from the serpent's root will come forth an adder, and its fruit will be a flying serpent. (Isa. 14:29)

Isaiah was warning the Philistines not to rejoice at their apparent liberation . As the German scholar Joachim Begrich pointed out, this did not refer to Ahaz but to Tiglath-pileser, king of Assyria, who had smitten the Philistines a great deal.[4] The Assyrian rod was broken—Tiglath-pileser was such an extraordinary figure, there was a belief that no successor could possibly be his equal in conquest—but the prophet Isaiah warned that in its wake would come an adder, the offspring of that snake, its fruit a "flying serpent." In other words, Assyria would not disappear from the scene. Assyria would continue to oppress the peoples of the area. The future serpentine rulers would be Tiglath-pileser's fruits—that is, his son and grandson.

I consequently propose removing the vision of the birth of the child and the defeat of the enemy from the immediate historical context. Like the prominent bible scholar Brevard Childs, I read it as a typological declaration of the greatest significance.[5] Isaiah had despaired of Ahaz and, generally speaking, had lost faith in the existing monarchs of the house of David. In his deep disappointment, he came to the conclusion that he could no longer praise the kings of the Davidic line, as had been done in the Psalms and in various prophecies. The present monarchy had failed, and one had to hope for the future appearance of a different, wondrous figure: the child who would be born.

Here one finds for the first time the idea that one day in the near or distant future an exalted figure would appear who would restore the greatness of the house of David, bring "peace without end" to the land, and establish the throne for all eternity. This, then, was the moment of the birth of messianic expectation. The bitter disappointment with the present, with King Ahaz who had renounced Judah's independence and become a vassal of the king of Assyria, had given rise to the hope of a wondrous future king who would restore things to their former glory.

We do not know how far off this future was for Isaiah when he made this prophecy. One can assume he hoped it would happen in his lifetime. But the great importance of the prophecy does not lie in the time of its fulfillment, but in the decision to look away from the present toward a redeeming figure who would appear at some time in the future.

It should be noted that the future redeeming figure was not a warrior. The defeat of Assyria would be the work of God, and only after that would the future king ascend the throne and impose his rule. As the great Israeli Bible scholar Yehezkel Kaufmann rightly said, in delineating the task of the messianic figure, Isaiah deeply influenced biblical messianic thought.[6] From that time forward until the end of the biblical period, there was no expectation that the messianic figure would fight battles and win wars. In accordance with his distrust of human power and his tendency to depend on the power of the divinity, Isaiah transferred the political and military aspects of the Messiah to God. The messianic figure, who appears after the enemy's defeat, has a different task: to bring justice, righteousness, and peace to the land.

The titles of the future king, given in 9:5, help us to gain deeper insight into the nature of this figure as Isaiah understood him. The title "Wonderful Counselor" describes him as an excellent adviser, extraordinarily wise. But how are we to understand the title "Everlasting Father," and the most audacious, "Mighty God"? In what sense can the future king be God? How can one give a man of flesh and blood the title "Mighty God"? Furthermore, does the title "Everlasting Father" suggest that the king the prophet hoped for would have eternal life? Aren't humans mortal by definition, and isn't God the only being to whom the Bible ascribes eternal existence?

Indeed, from the time of the Second Temple and the sages until today, these verses have troubled readers and commentators, some of whom have suggested that these words do not describe the future child, but God. Yet, in fact, in these descriptions Isaiah was not saying anything new. A reading of a few psalms demonstrates that his prophecy was based on existing biblical traditions.

Psalm 45, which concerns a marriage of a king of Israel to a princess from Tyre, is connected with the kingdom of Israel in its days of greatness and splendor, at some moment before the end of the eighth century BCE. The Psalmist describes the king as "the fairest of the sons of men; grace is poured upon your lips; therefore God has blessed you for ever" (Ps. 45:2). To the king's possession of grace, beauty, and God's blessing the Psalmist adds warlike valor:

> Gird your sword upon your thigh, O mighty
>   one, in your glory and majesty!
> In your majesty ride forth victoriously
> for the cause of truth and to defend the right; let
>   your right hand teach you dread deeds!
> Your arrows are sharp in the heart of the king's enemies;
> the peoples fall under you. (Ps. 45:3–5)

The psalm continues:

> Your throne, God, endures for ever and ever.
> The royal scepter is a scepter of equity;
> you love righteousness and hate wickedness,
> therefore God, your God, has anointed you with the
>   oil of gladness above your fellows. (Ps. 45:6–7)

According to 45:7, the king's love of righteousness is the reason why he is anointed by God. And because verse 7 describes the king, we have no alternative but to regarding the audacious words in verse 6—"Your throne, God, endures for ever and ever"—as also referring to the king. The Psalmist calls the king "God," and says that his throne is everlasting. As in the prophecies of Isaiah, a king, as a ruler, is tasked with establishing justice and righteousness in the realm—and, as with Isaiah, the king is called "God" and endowed with immortality.

In some other psalms, we see a similar elevation of the king, and in certain cases he is also given eternal life. Psalm 21 praises a king:

> In thy strength the king rejoices, O Lord;
> and in thy help how greatly he exults!

Thou hast given him his heart's desire, and hast
   not withheld the request of his lips. Selah.
   (21:1–2; *selah* is probably a mark directing the
   singers of the psalm to raise their voices).

Further on, the Psalmist elaborates on the king's relationship
with God: "He asked life of thee; thou gavest it to him, length
of days for ever and ever" (21:4). Likewise, in Psalm 61 we read:
"Prolong the life of the king; may his years endure to all generations! May he be enthroned for ever before God; bid steadfast
love and faithfulness watch over him!" (61:6–7).

Our book of Psalms is a collection of songs from various generation. Some are very old, from the premonarchic era. Some
are from the monarchic period—and possibly several songs in
this group were indeed composed by David (legend credits him
with having composed them all). Other psalms are later, exilic or
postexilic. The Royal Psalms, which were composed in the kingdoms of Judah and Israel, usually praise the current king of Judah
or Israel. Psalm 45, quoted above, was probably written for the
wedding of King Ahab and the Princess Jezebel, daughter of the
king of Tyre and Sidon (see Psalm 45:13, 1 Kings 16:31). Isaiah,
who lived 150 years after Ahab, could very well have known about
this psalm and other Royal Psalms composed before and during
his time. It seems that he borrowed ideas that were in existence
before his time—ideas in the Psalms connected with contemporary
kings—and transferred them to the future, to the new messianic
figure he conceived.

It should be noted that Isaiah's prophecy does not specifically
mention the word "Messiah" (the anointed one), whereas in Psalm
45:7 God anoints the king with oil as a reward for his righteousness: "You love righteousness and hate wickedness. Therefore
God, your God, has anointed you with the oil of gladness above
your fellows." Elsewhere too in the Bible the word "Messiah" is

connected with the anointing with oil, the pouring of olive oil on the king's head. Among the examples are the coronations of the first Israelite king Saul ("Then Samuel took a vial of oil and poured it on his head and kissed him and said, Has not the Lord anointed you to be prince over Israel?" 1 Sam. 10:1) and of David ("Then Samuel took the horn of oil and anointed him in the midst of his brothers," 1 Sam. 16:13).

As we can learn from an ancient text from the city of Mari, one of the early sources in which we encounter the anointment ritual, the significance of this ritual seems to be connected with the splendor and light bestowed on the body by the anointing. The anointing of the king with shining oil makes him like God, who was originally conceived as enveloped in light, and gives him a godlike splendor.

Composed in the eighteenth century BCE, in the ancient royal city of Mari on the River Euphrates, close to the present-day border between Syria and Iraq, this ancient document, written six hundred years before the formation of Israel, relates the words of a prophet sent to a king by the storm god Hadad:

> I have placed you on the throne of your father's house, I have given you the weapons with which I fought against Tiamat [a mythical dragon], I have anointed you with the oil of my splendor, and thus no one can stand up to you. I have bestowed on you the divine splendor and the divine weapons of war.
>
> Pay heed to this word when a litigant cries out against you. Judge him fairly, answer him honestly.[7]

It is clear from the Mari text that the ritual of anointment with olive oil has a deep symbolic meaning. The oil causes the skin to shine. The shining skin of the anointed king is a symbol of the divine splendor that was bestowed upon him.

The god Hadad reminds the king that he is successful in war only because he is anointed with the oil of his splendor, and tells him that this obliges him to pursue righteousness and justice. If in Psalm 45 righteousness and justice serve as the rationale for the anointing, here we have the opposite—they are the consequence of the anointing—but nonetheless in both cases there is a deep connection between the two. We find a similar connection in the prophecy of Isaiah, who associates the "divine" king with the justice and righteousness he will bring to the land.

And so while the particular word "Messiah" and the ritual of anointing that appear in the Psalms and in the biblical descriptions of coronations are missing from Isaiah's prophecies, nevertheless I call the prophecy we have been dealing with a messianic prophecy, for I understand messianism to mean the expectation of an exalted figure who will appear in the future and establish "justice, righteousness and peace without end." A figure of this kind is at the heart of many biblical prophecies that, even if they do not speak specifically of a Messiah, anticipate the notion that in the course of Jewish history will come to be called the messianic idea.

The year 733 BCE was a year of reverses and a turning point. On the one hand, it was the beginning of the physical destruction of the kingdom of Israel and the political destruction of the kingdom of Judah, connected with its loss of independence. On the other hand, precisely because of the gravity of the crisis and Isaiah's deep disappointment, it gave rise to Isaiah's biblical idea of the expectation of a future messianic figure. He was a king given the name of God and endowed with eternal life—"Wonderful Counselor, Mighty God, Eternal Father, Prince of Peace"—an exalted superhuman figure who aspired to divinity.

Concurrently, at the very same period in which Isaiah was making his prophecies in Judah, the prophet Hosea, living in the kingdom of Israel, arrived at an entirely different understanding of these events. The conflict between two divergent Hebrew visions would be at full throttle about 770 years later, when the Pharisees (spiritual ancestors of the rabbinic sages) and Sadducees fought over ideas of divine providence and a semidivine Messiah, and Sadducee judges sentenced Jesus to death.

But first, it is to the Israelite prophet Hosea's repudiation of a messianic vision that we now turn.

2

Rejection of the Kingship Concept

At roughly the same time that Isaiah announced the appearance of a future godlike royal figure, "Mighty God, Everlasting Father," Hosea preached the very opposite message about kingship.

Both prophets shared a profound sense of disappointment with the existing kings of their lands, but came to opposite conclusions about messianism and kingship. Isaiah, as we saw, remained loyal to the house of David, but out of his disappointment with the existing kings he raised expectations of a wondrous figure in the future who would sit on the throne of David and bring justice and righteousness to the land. On the other hand, disappointment with the kings of his time led Hosea (who started his prophetic activity some fifteen years earlier) to adamantly reject the institution of monarchy and call for its total prohibition.

The two prophets' divergent judgments can largely be attributed to differences in their locales. Isaiah prophesied in Jerusalem, in the kingdom of Judah. There he was heir to a more than 250-year tradition in which the dynasty of the house of David had sat on the Jerusalem throne, one king after another, without a break (with the brief exception of the period of Queen Athaliah). Around the dynasty of the house of David a special aura derived from the figure of David, the promises he and succeeding kings had received from God, and belief in the continuity and perpetuity of the dynasty. All this conveyed a strong message of confidence and faith—not in each king personally, but in the importance and sanctity of the dynasty, which enjoyed the favor of God. Isaiah would have known all this, either from the Psalms or from other literary traditions passed on through word of mouth.

On the other hand, in the Northern Kingdom, Israel, where Hosea preached, there was no continuous dynasty, and not even a fixed capital.[1] Dynasties succeeded one another—and in Hosea's time, with ever-increasing frequency. During the twenty-five years of Hosea's activity (750–725 BCE) no fewer than nine kings reigned in Israel, four of them murdered by insurgents. The unstable nature of these dynasties would have conferred little assurance as to their ultimate continuity. Furthermore, no dynasty in the Northern Kingdom managed to acquire significant religious aura, making strong criticism of the very institution of kingship all the more likely.

To all this must be added the fact that Hosea lived and worked after the end of the great age of the kingdom of Israel.

Hosea began prophesying at the end of the reign of Jeroboam II, somewhere around 750 BCE, and most likely he ceased prophesying immediately before the destruction of Samaria (capital of the Northern Kingdom) in 725 BCE. In the first half of the eighth century BCE, Jeroboam II, ruling in the kingdom of Israel, had extended the kingdom's borders more than any other king, through conquests beyond the Jordan and in the Golan Heights. By the end of the period of his rule, however, the rise of Assyria under Tiglath-pileser III had begun—an ascendance that would ultimately lead to the destruction of the kingdom of Israel. Thus Hosea was active in a period of deterioration and—one thing leading to another—the political disintegration increased instability in the kingdom, encouraging internal insurrections and the replacement of kings. All in all, the general decline of the kingdom left the kingdom in distress.

The period had another political characteristic that brings us to the subject of Hosea's prophecies: the search for strong external allies. The confusion and weakness of the kingdom of Israel forced it to turn intermittently to the two great powers of the age: the ancient superpower of Egypt and the ascendant empire of Assyria: "They make a bargain with Assyria, and oil is carried to Egypt" (Hosea 12:1).

To Hosea, the kingdom of Israel's dependence on human allies showed that it did not rely on God, and in fact was unfaithful to God. He railed against Israel's alliances as a political and religious betrayal:

Calling to Egypt, going to Assyria. . . . Woe to them, for they have strayed from me! Destruction to them, for they have rebelled against me! (Hosea 7:11,13)

Hosea further denounced the pacts as prostitution with the nations. He likened the alliance with Assyria to sexual relations with a strange lover:

For they have gone up to Assyria . . . Ephraim has hired lovers. (Hosea 8:9)

Since Ephraim was the main tribe among the ten tribes that formed the Northern Kingdom of Israel, Hosea referred to this kingdom as "Ephraim." He blamed Ephraim for having "hired" lovers as one pays a prostitute. The payment is the tax that the kings of Israel had to pay to the Assyrian emperors who subjugated them.

For better or worse, many of Hosea's theological concepts are taken from the sexual realm, and perhaps that is connected to the personal life of the prophet. Unlike Isaiah, who appears to have had a good and harmonious marriage (we know very little about his wife, but she was called a "prophetess," either because she was actually a female prophet or because she was the wife of a prophet), Hosea had an unusual married life. In a very surprising manner, the book of Hosea opens with God's command to Hosea to marry a prostitute, and chapter 3 relates another story of his marriage to a prostitute. Whether it was the same woman or two different ones, unfaithfulness and prostitution were painful subjects for Hosea, and one may assume this influenced the metaphors and images he chose to describe the relations between the people of Israel and their God.

Yet a deeper examination of Hosea's prophecies reveals that he not only regarded dependence on a foreign people and alliance with a foreign country as prostitution, but he looked on the very existence of a monarchy in Israel in a similar way. To Hosea, dependence on an Israelite king and his military power constituted another unfaithfulness to God.

We see this in a few verses in chapter 3, which opens with an order "to love a woman who is beloved of a paramour and is an adulteress." Hosea relates how he purchased her and the price he paid, and then said to her: "You must dwell as mine for many days; you shall not play the harlot, or belong to another man; so will I also be to you" (Hosea 3:3). In other words, because he had purchased her, he had the right to expect her to be sexually faithful to him alone. He tells her to remain alone for a long time, without partaking in acts of prostitution, and also without sexual relations with him. This, Hosea proceeds to say in the succeeding verse, exemplified or symbolized the relation of the people of Israel to their God: "For the children of Israel shall dwell many days without king or prince, without sacrifice or pillar, without ephod or teraphim" (3:4).[2]

How is this verse to be understood? The words "ephod or teraphim" were taken from forbidden rites. Teraphim were images of ancestors, which people fed in order to help them divine the future, on the understanding that the dead knew what was going to happen next. The people laid food at the feet of idols. Thus in the story of Saul at En Dor, the spirit of the dead Samuel informed Saul of his forthcoming defeat and death at the hands of the Philistines (1 Sam. 28:13–19; see also Isa. 8:9). As for the ephod Hosea mentions, we do not know exactly what it was, but it also seems to have been connected with divining the future, and it is mentioned next to the teraphim elsewhere (Judg. 17:5).

To "ephod or teraphim" Hosea added "sacrifice" and "pillar," two perfectly acceptable items of divine worship, at least for the people of the Northern Kingdom. In the stories of the Patriarchs, the pillar appears as part of a quite legitimate ritual: Jacob set up pillars at Bethel and Gilead (Gen. 28:18, 32:45). (Later, however, the book of Deuteronomy would forbid its use.[3])

In effect, Hosea placed pagan elements side by side with legitimate elements in order to pass a negative sentence on the entirety of rituals, including divine sacrifice. The denigration of sacrifice appears again and again in Hosea's prophecy. "For I desire steadfast love and not sacrifice, the knowledge of God, rather than burnt offerings" (Hosea 6:6). Elsewhere, he describes the people going to seek God and bringing sacrifices, but they do not find God, who has disappeared: "With their flocks and herds they shall go to seek the Lord, but they will not find him; he has withdrawn from them" (5:6).

Now, if we return to the verse in its entirety—"For the children of Israel shall dwell many days without king or prince, without sacrifice or pillar, without ephod or teraphim" (Hosea 3:4)—we can observe another surprising element within it. Next to the sacrifice and pillar, the ephod and teraphim, we find a king and prince. In other words, just like ritual, Hosea is rejecting the monarchical regime.

Hosea's rationale is spelled out in another verse: "They made kings, but not through me, they set up princes, but without my knowledge. With their silver and gold they made idols for their own destruction" (Hosea 8:4). Here, he lumps kings and princes together with silver and gold with which Israel fashions idols. God condemns idolatry. The coronation is not according to God's will. The uplifting of kings and princes is invalid like the fashioning of gold and silver idols.

Chapter 13 of the book of Hosea offers us a deeper understanding of the prophet's opposition to the institution of kingship among the people of Israel. The chapter begins with a condemnation of foreign or false rituals. After condemning the worship of Baal, the Canaanite god of fertility (in 13:1), Hosea declares:

And now they sin more and more, and make for themselves molten images, idols skillfully made of their silver, all of them the work of craftsmen. It is said of these people, "They offer human sacrifices and kiss the calf-idols." (13:2)

Here again are idols of silver, but with the clarification that they are calves. These are the two golden calves that Jeroboam I, son of Nebat, set up in the two main temples of the kingdom of Israel, in Bethel and Dan. Hosea is accusing Israel of kissing these calves.

After condemning this idolatry, Hosea, clearly hinting at the first two of the Ten Commandments, says: "I am the Lord your God from the land of Egypt; you know no God but me, and besides me there is no savior" (Hosea 13:4). And a few verses further on, Hosea broaches the subject of kingship:

Where is now your king to save you; where are all your princes to defend you—those of whom you said, 'Give me a king and princes'? I have given you kings in my anger, and I have taken them away in my wrath. (13:10–11).

As some commentators have suggested, these verses may be connected with the story in the book of Samuel in which the people ask Samuel to give them a king.[4] The statement "Give me a king and princes" echoes the words of the elders of Israel to Samuel: "Now appoint for us a king to govern us like all the nations" (1 Sam. 8:5). Samuel did not approve of the people's demand, and when he turned to God he received a clear answer:

Hearken to the voice of the people in all that they say to you; for they have not rejected you, but they have rejected me from being king over them. According to all the deeds which they have done to me, from the day I brought them up out of Egypt even to this day, forsaking me and serving other gods, so they are also doing to you. (1 Sam. 8:7–8)

God tells Samuel that the demand was not directed against him but against God. God likens the people's insistence on a king to idolatry: just as Israel had been unfaithful to God in worshiping idols, so the people were now rejecting God as a leader and seeking God's replacement in a king of flesh and blood. A few chapters later, Samuel states this clearly:

> Thus saith the Lord, the God of Israel, "I brought up Israel out of Egypt, and I delivered you from the hand of the Egyptians and from the hand of all the kingdoms that were oppressing you. But you have this day rejected your God, who saves you from all your calamities and your distresses; and you have said, 'No! But set a king over us.'" (1 Sam. 10:18–19)

From Hosea we hear a very similar criticism of the institution of monarchy: "I have given you kings in my anger and I have taken them away in my wrath." No doubt, he was hinting at the rapid replacement of the occupiers of the throne. As was mentioned above, in the twenty-five years or so in which Hosea was active, seven different kings reigned in Israel; four of the seven would be murdered by insurgents making violent assault on the throne.

Thus from the start Hosea clearly rules out the demand for a king: "Besides me there is no savior" (Hosea 13:4). God is the sole deliverer. Not only other gods, but also kings of flesh and blood cannot save the people. As this is the case, the people's expectation that a king of flesh and blood can save them is a sin like idolatry.

It is probable that Hosea was familiar with antimonarchical traditions like the one reflected in the book of Samuel and the one in the story of the judge Gideon, who refused Israel's request to him to rule over them ("I will not rule over you, and my son will not rule over you; the Lord will rule over you," Judg. 8:23). These parts of the books of Samuel and Judges were written in the Northern Kingdom more or less in the time of Hosea, who likely would have read them or heard about them through word of mouth, and been inspired by them as well.

The first prophet to depict God and Israel as a married couple, Hosea described the wonderful beginnings of their married life in the time of the people's wanderings in the desert, until they arrived on the threshold of the Promised Land and committed the sin of worshiping the Canaanite Baal Pe'or, possibly in a ritual that included sexual elements.[5] Israel was like an unfaithful wife who took on lovers; she mistakenly thought that the gifts she received from her husband—agricultural produce, fruit, and wool—were provided by her lover, Baal. As a result, God confronted Israel as an adulterous spouse, stripping her and humiliating her, until God finally took her to a dwelling in the desert where they spent a honeymoon and renewed their marriage vows: "And I will betroth you to me for ever; I will betroth you to me in righteousness and in justice, in steadfast love, and in mercy. I will betroth you to me in faithfulness; and you shall know the Lord" (Hosea 2:19–20).

In the background of this marriage drama is a violent controversy about who is responsible for giving fertility to the land: the God of Israel or Baal, the Canaanite fertility god. One can sense this particularly in the prophecy that in the future, "You will call me 'my husband,' and no longer will you call me, 'My Baal'" (Hosea 2:16). But there is another, less visible level of meaning here that archaeological findings of the last decades can help us to recognize. Inscriptions found in the areas of Beit Guvrin (near Hebron) and Sinai speak of a blessing in the name of "Yahweh and his Asherah," a combination of the God of Israel and the Asherah, the sacred tree symbolizing the goddess Asherah. These inscriptions attribute the blessing to the marriage between God—the Lord—and the goddess Asherah. Another inscription, found on the island of Elephantine in Upper Egypt (thought to belong to a settlement of Jewish mercenaries in the Persian army who came from the kingdom of Israel), shows the combination "Anat-Yahu." Anat was a "younger" goddess than Asherah, belonging to the generation of her daughters. Ancient myths depict her as a warrior goddess loyal to Baal who fought for his dominion. It seems that these soldiers in Egypt thought it was better for "Yahu," the God of Israel, to be matched with Anat than with Asherah.

Views of this kind likely formed the background to Hosea's harsh statements. From his point of view, it was inconceivable that God could have physical union and offspring like other gods such as Baal. God did in fact have a partner in marriage, but the partner was not a pagan deity. God's partner was metaphoric: the people of Israel.

This hidden controversy permits us to gain a better understanding of the enigmatic verses that end the book of Hosea. Already before the archaeological discoveries about God and his consort, scholars had suggested a fascinating emendation of the reading of these verses, later confirmed retroactively by the findings. In these verses, God asks the people of Israel: "O Ephraim, what have I to do with idols?" In other words, why do you still worship images? And God adds: "It is I who answer and look after you [*ani aniti veashurenu*]. I am like an evergreen cypress, from me comes your fruit" (Hosea 14:8). Scholars had been perplexed by the meaning of the words *ani aniti veashurenu*, which form an irregular sentence with no parallel elsewhere in the Bible. The scholar Julius Wellhausen suggested emending the verse to read, "I am his Anat and his Asherah [*ani Anato ve-Asherato*]"—that is to say, "You do not need to turn to idols, to the goddesses Anat and Asherah, and marry them to God: 'I am his Anat and his Asherah!'"[6] The female aspect of God is within me, and "from me comes your fruit." All blessing and fertility come from me: they are not the product of a marriage between God and a goddess.

Under this interpretation, in Hosea's view God was "married" to a collective partner, the people of Israel, and God had children by her. But these were not biological children, and this was not a physical union. The children were the Israelites: "When Israel was a child I loved him, and out of Egypt I called my son" (Hosea 11:1).

In effect, Hosea transferred all the images concerning the God-Israel relationship from the sphere of a king and his subjects to that of the family. God was not a king; God was a lover or a father.

We do not know what happened to Hosea after the kingdom of Israel fell to the Assyrians, but somehow or other his prophecies reached Jerusalem—one may assume in scrolls he or one of his disciples had written. But once his prophecies reached Judah, they did not remain as they were. The Judeans who read the angry prophecies about Ephraim and Judah were apparently not very pleased with them. Thus, as happens to texts that pass from hand to hand, verses in Hosea appear to have been changed here and there to the advantage of the members of the kingdom of Judah. Here are three examples of emendations of this kind.

1. In the first chapter, Hosea says: "She conceived again and bore a daughter. And the Lord said to him, 'Call her name Not Pitied, for I will no more have pity on the house of Israel'" (Hosea 1:6). The natural continuation of these words appears in verse 8: "When she had weaned Not Pitied, she conceived and bore a son." But between these two verses, a Judean editor seems to have intervened to tone down the prophecy: "But I will have pity on the house of Judah, and I will deliver them by the Lord their God; I will not deliver them by bow, nor by sword, nor by war, nor by horses, nor by horsemen" (1:7). Although a deliverance "not by bow, nor by sword, nor by war" was very much in keeping with Hosea's ideology, the Israelite prophet was not overly concerned with what would happen to the house of Judah, referring to it only on rare occasions. Therefore, these words, which break the continuity of the text, seem to be a later addition.

2. At the end of chapter 1, Hosea says "And the people of Judah and the people of Israel shall be gathered together" (1:11). In all other places where Hosea mentions Judah and

Israel, he gives Israel precedence over Judah, so this sole case in which the order is reversed arouses suspicion. The suspicion is confirmed by the content of the prophecy: "And they shall appoint for themselves one head: and they shall go up from the land" (1:11). These words are not suited to Hosea, the prophet who did not want a head, a leader, or a king, and who asked for trust to be placed in God alone.

3. At the end of chapter 3, following the prophecy "For the children of Israel shall dwell many days without king or prince" (3:4), Hosea says, "Afterward the children of Israel shall return and seek the Lord their God, and David their king; and they shall come in fear to the Lord and to his goodness in the latter days" (3:5). Nearly all commentators believe that the words "and David their king" represent a later addition by a Judean editor. Hosea gave no importance to King David, and, as we have seen, rejected kingship in general. Furthermore, the term "the latter days" was characteristic of Judean literature, and doesn't otherwise appear in the prophecies of Hosea or Amos (another Northern Kingdom prophet), bolstering the "later addition" thesis.

If we remove these later additions from the prophecies of Hosea, we discover a prophet strongly opposed to any reliance on human power, whether that of a foreign country or of an Israelite king. In his opinion, the only savior was God: "And besides me there is no savior" (Hosea 13:4). From here he reached the extreme conception that not only repudiates as kind of idolatry any reliance on a king, whether Israelite or foreign, but also rejects the royal imagery of God.

This is the most antimonarchical position to be found in the Bible and, as we have said, it appeared simultaneously with the monarchical-messianic pronouncements of Isaiah, or slightly earlier. These very impressive initial affirmations of two opposing biblical views would continue to develop in various circuitous ways throughout biblical literature and beyond.

Relevant to this discussion of Hosea's antimonarchical approach is a text that appears to have been written at the same time and place as the book of Hosea, and was even inspired by him, and which also reached Jerusalem, where it was rewritten to some extent. I am referring here to the original nucleus of the book of Deuteronomy, which, as scholars like Martin Noth and Harold L. Ginsburg have seen, had its origins in the Northern Kingdom and was highly influenced by Hosea's prophesies.[7]

The northern origins of Deuteronomy are especially revealed by the great importance the text ascribes to the making of the covenant on Mount Gerizim and Mount Ebal—both in the Northern Kingdom. Deuteronomy's main body of laws appears between chapter 11 and chapter 26, surrounded by the covenant. Immediately before it, the final verses of chapter 11 relate the making of the covenant on Mount Gerizim and Mount Ebal, and immediately after it, the first verses of chapter 27 continue to describe the making of the covenant between these mountains. It is very hard to believe that a writer from the Southern Kingdom of Judah would have given such weight to the northern Mounts Gerizim and Ebal.

Hosea, like Amos, lived in the eighth century BCE in the north. Archaeological findings tell us that this was the first period in which literacy started to spread among the inhabitants of the Northern Kingdom. This is the reason why the prophecies of Elijah, who lived one hundred years earlier, were not recorded: there was no literate public to read them!

Deuteronomy was originally composed for the people of Israel about the same time as Hosea. It was intended for all the people, not just an elite of priestly scribes. For the first time, in the middle of the eighth century, there were significant numbers of literate people in the kingdom who could read and appreciate this book.

As such, the original nucleus of the book appears to have been written in the Northern Kingdom in the time of Hosea, and it somehow reached Jerusalem. Chapters 22–23 of 2 Kings relate how about a hundred years after the destruction of Samaria, when King Josiah was reigning in Judah, the priest Hilkiah found a "book of the law" in the Temple and brought it to the king. Following the book's discovery, Josiah made a sweeping reform of the Temple rituals. The German scholar De Wette suggested that this "book of the law" was none other than the book of Deuteronomy, and that suggestion has become one of the cornerstones of modern biblical scholarship.

Like Hosea, the book of Deuteronomy refrains from describing God in terms of kingship (except for once, in Moses' blessing on the tribes, which is not in the original main part of the book). Like Hosea, Deuteronomy depicts God as a father—"You are the sons of the Lord your God" (Deut. 14:1)—and it also seems to be aware of the metaphor of love and marriage. Concerning the election—the reason why God chose the people of Israel, specifically—it says: if "the Lord has chosen you to be a people for his own possession, out of all the peoples that are on the face of the earth" (Deut. 14:2), "it was not because you were more in number than any other people that the Lord set his love [*hashak*] upon you and chose you, for you were the fewest of all peoples, but it is because the Lord loves you" (Deut. 7:7). There were good reasons for God to have chosen a large, strong nation like Egypt, Assyria, or Babylon. The reason God turned to a small nation like Israel instead was love. God loved Israel, and love cannot be questioned. The word *hashak*, which has an erotic connotation in the Bible, also appears elsewhere in Deuteronomy in this connection: "The Lord set his heart in love [*hashak*] upon your fathers and chose their descendants after them, you, above all peoples, as at this day" (Deut. 10:15).

The book of Deuteronomy seems to have followed Hosea's example in describing the relationship between God and Israel as one of fatherhood or erotic love. Also like Hosea, it was unsympathetic to the institution of monarchy and to reliance on military force.

Unlike him, however, the book of Deuteronomy could not say this in an aggressive manner. While Deuteronomy was rooted in the northern circles, which totally rejected the idea of kingship, the book was ultimately published in Jerusalem, the seat of the house of David, where the institution of monarchy could not be completely deplored. Deuteronomy therefore gave a king a place in its laws, but an examination of the laws concerning a king (Deut. 17:14–20) reveals a strange character. The initial verse of this passage is already formulated in a curious way:

> When you come to the land which the Lord your God gives you, and you possess it and dwell in it, and then say, "I will set a king over me, like all the nations that are round about me. . . ." (17:14)

This is not like a regular commandment of Deuteronomy to do such and such. The people of Israel are not commanded to appoint a king. Rather, the text functions only as a reply to the people's request to have a king like all other nations. The words clearly echo the first biblical account of a coronation, in the book of Samuel, which says that the king was not chosen on God's orders but in response to the people's demand for "a king like all the nations" (1 Sam. 8:5).

The laws of kingship in the book of Deuteronomy begin in a tone of reserve. There is no divine commandment to appoint a king. Nothing is said about his anointment. From there, most of the subsequent laws serve to restrict, prohibit, and otherwise circumscribe the king. The king is forbidden to multiply horses, to multiply wives, and to amass silver and gold (Deut. 17:16–17). Thus, while a king may be appointed, he cannot amass a large army or the financial means to enlarge his army. In fact, as Ginsburg has pointed out, he is a king without a regular army.[8]

This explains the statement in the Deuteronomic laws concerning warfare: "When you go forth to war against your enemies, and see horses and chariots, and an army larger than your own, you shall not be afraid of them; for the Lord your God is with you, who brought you up out of the land of Egypt" (Deut. 20:1). The enemy has horses and chariots, but the people of Israel do not have them; their only deliverer is God.

As Ginsburg has shown, this approach to an army and the institution of kingship also explains the law by which officers exempt various people from participating in a war: the man who has built a house and has not dedicated it, the man who has planted a vineyard and has not enjoyed its fruit, or simply "the man who is fearful and fainthearted" (Deut. 20:8). The army described here is obviously not a professional one, as were those of the neighboring kingdoms. Neither a man who is "fearful and fainthearted" nor a man who had planted a vineyard would be considered for a professional army. The soldiers in such an army would be wage-earners and would not make their living from agriculture. But if the king is not allowed to multiply horses or silver and gold, he would not have the money to pay wages or keep a regular army. Rather, he would have a kind of "people's army," an army of volunteers like that described in the period of the judges. The song of Deborah twice praises the volunteers (Judg. 5:2,9). These were plain farmers who left their fields to defend their tribe and nation out of their own volition, without expecting or receiving any payment.

Ginsburg holds that Deuteronomy's portrayal of the king and his army represents a practical implementation of the principles Hosea affirmed in his prophecies. The laws of Deuteronomy do not allow one to imagine that deliverance can come from an army, horses, or chariots. God is the deliverer, and all hopes for victory in war must be placed in God.

As was mentioned, unlike the tradition in other biblical books, the king of Deuteronomy is not anointed with oil, and unlike Saul, David, and Solomon (see 1 Sam. 13:9, 2 Sam. 6:12–19, 1 Kings 8:63), he has no role or status in religious ceremonies. Moreover, he does not even lead the army, for, according to Deuteronomy, those that go before the camp and encourage the people to fight are God's representatives, the priests (Deut. 20:1–4). Furthermore, the king plays no part in the legal system, in total contrast to the point of view in the Psalms and the prophecies of Isaiah, which particularly stress the king's role in imposing "righteousness and justice." In fact, the decision in a complicated legal and cultic problem is given to the priests or to the judges, and not to the king. (See Deut. 17:8–11).

One might then ask: What should the king do after all these responsibilities are taken from him? Deuteronomy's answer is simple: let him sit and study the Torah. "And when he sits on the throne of his kingdom, he shall write for himself in a book a copy of this law, from that which is in charge of the Levitical priests; and it will be with him, and he shall read in it all the days of his life, that he may learn to fear the Lord his God, by keeping all the words of this law and these statutes, by doing them; that his heart may not be lifted above his brethren, and that he may not turn aside from the commandment, either to the right hand or to the left" (Deut. 17:18–20).

The fact that the king has no role in ceremonies, in the army, or in the legal system seems designed to ensure that he will have no sense of superiority, "that his heart may not be lifted above his brethren." A king of this kind is in total contrast to the wondrous and lofty figure depicted in Isaiah's prophecies. While Isaiah strives to elevate the king as much as possible, to the point of calling him "Mighty God, Eternal Father," the book of Deuteronomy seeks to diminish the king's image as much as possible, largely by making him powerless to rule. In so doing, the book of Deuteronomy can be read as an extension of Hosea's view that the people must place their trust in God alone.

Thus, the encounter with the harsh reality of the decline of the kingdom, the loss of autonomy, and the untrustworthy monarchy gave rise to two contrary reactions. Isaiah despaired of the present and turned to the future, to a future redeeming figure. He produced the initial version of the messianic idea and glorified a future monarchy, the object of his hopes. Hosea, in the face of similar disappointment, renounced the institution of kingship and sought to return to the period four hundred years earlier when judges ruled the Land of Israel. There was obviously no place for messianism here: the only redeemer was God.

Deuteronomy was the first book of the Torah to be published for the entire people. Its skeptical attitude toward the king would come to be shared by the other four books of Moses. Neither in Deuteronomy nor in the other books of the Torah can we find any eschatological or messianic expectation. One cannot establish any Jewish messianic group on this basis.

When we later meet the judges of Jesus, priests, and scribes, it is important to remember that they were raised and educated mainly on the antimonarchic and antimessianic conceptions of the Torah.

3

Reconceiving the Messiah

By the second half of the seventh century BCE, about a hundred years after the prophecies of Isaiah and Hosea, the prophet Jeremiah was active in Judah. His prophecies began around 627 BCE, in the time of King Josiah, and continued until a few years after the Temple's destruction in 586 BCE, when he was taken to Egypt (see Jer. 1:1–3; 40:1–44:30). Jeremiah would extend the messianic idea in the direction of Isaiah—and he was even more extreme.

Isaiah, as we saw, had called the future messianic figure "Wonderful Counselor, Mighty God"—an audacious appellation. Jeremiah furthermore proclaimed:

> Behold, the days are coming, says the Lord, when I will raise up for David a righteous Branch, and he shall reign as king and deal wisely, and shall execute justice and righteousness in the land. In his days Judah will be saved, and Israel will dwell securely. And this is the name by which he will be called: YHWH is our righteousness. (Jer. 23:5–6)

Jeremiah's words "righteous Branch" recall Isaiah's prophecy that a shoot would appear from the root of the kingdom of the house of David: "There shall come forth a shoot from the stump of Jesse, and a branch shall grow out of his roots" (Isa. 11:1). The expression "righteous branch" is also found in Phoenician inscriptions of the fifth and sixth centuries BCE, where it means a legal heir to the throne, the legitimate ("righteous") offspring of the king. Perhaps here, too, there is an echo of this meaning.

But first and foremost, the words "righteous branch" appear within a passage that stresses the importance of the word "righteous," by repeating it in various ways three times. Most intriguingly, Jeremiah tells us, "And this is the name by which he will be called: 'the Lord our righteousness.'" And so, whereas Isaiah had called the future king "Mighty God," Jeremiah, active a century later, went even further, prophesying that this king would be given God's own name: "YHWH is our righteousness."

These audacious words, which give the most sacred name of God—YHWH—to an earthly human king, were already regarded as problematic close to the time when Jeremiah said them. This is proven by the insertion of a subsequent passage in the Hebrew version of the book of Jeremiah itself—a passage missing in the old Greek (Septuagint) version:

> Behold, the days are coming, says the Lord, when I will fulfill the promise I made to the house of Israel and the house of Judah. In those days and at that time I will cause a righteous Branch to spring forth for David; and he shall execute justice and righteousness in the land. In those days Judah will be saved and Jerusalem will dwell securely. *And this is the name by which it will be called: "YHWH is our righteousness."* (Jer. 33:14–16; italics added)

Here the title "YHWH is our righteousness" is not given to the future human king who would arise from the house of David, but to the city of Jerusalem. Here we do not have the problematic application of the most sacred name YHWH to an earthly king. Most likely, one of Jeremiah's disciples or successors wrote this prophecy to soften the bold statement of his master. As mentioned, this passage is missing from the Septuagint. Most scholars assume that the Greek translation of Jeremiah is based on a shorter and more original Hebrew version of the book. This supports the idea that these verses were added later to Jeremiah's original prophecy.

Why, then, did Jeremiah prophesy about a future king, "YHWH is our righteousness," who would execute righteousness and justice in the land? I believe this prophecy has to be seen against the background of his strong criticism of the contemporary kings of Judea. For example, we read in chapter 22:

> Hear the word of the Lord, O king of Judah, who sit on the throne of David. . . . Thus says the Lord: Do justice and righteousness, and deliver from the hand of the oppressor him who has been robbed. . . . For if you will indeed obey this word, then there shall enter the gates of this house kings who sit on the throne of David. . . . But if you will not heed these words, I swear by myself, says the Lord, that this house shall become a desolation. (22:2–5)

Jeremiah asked the kings to execute justice and righteousness, and threatened that if they failed to do so, the Temple would be destroyed. Further on, he rebuked certain kings, as in his criticism of Jehoiakim, the son of Josiah, who ruled from 609 to 598 BCE: "Woe to him that builds his house by unrighteousness, and his upper rooms by injustice" (Jer. 22:13). Describing the magnificent palace that Jehoiakim had built, which in Jeremiah's eyes was based on fortune gained in illegal ways, Jeremiah said that unlike Jehoiakim's father Josiah, who had reigned with justice and righteousness, "You have eyes and heart only for your dishonest gain, for shedding innocent blood, and for practicing oppression and violence" (22:17). Jeremiah also foresaw a very bad end for Jehoiakim:

> As I live, says the Lord, though Coniah, the son of Jehoiakim, king of Judah, were the signet ring on my right hand, yet I would tear you off and give you into the hand of those who seek your life, into the hand of those of whom you are afraid, even into the hand of Nebuchadnezzar king of Babylon and into the hand of the Chaldeans. I will hurl you and the mother who bore you into another country, where you were not born,

and there you shall die. But to the land to which they will long to return, there they shall not return. (22:24)

Indeed, in the final years of his reign, Jehoiakim would rebel against the Babylonian empire, and although he would die before King Nebuchadnezzar of Babylon reached the area, his son Jeconiah would reign for only three months before he was exiled to Babylon with the Jerusalem nobility in 597 BCE—an exile that would come to be known as "the exile of Jeconiah."

Jeremiah ended his prophecy with these bitter words:

O land, land, land, hear the word of the Lord! Thus says the Lord: "Write this man down as childless, a man who shall not succeed in his days; for none of his offspring shall succeed in sitting on the throne of David, and ruling again in Judah." (22:29–30)

That is to say, there would be no continuation of the royal line and Jeconiah would not have a successor.

In the end, things turned out slightly differently, for in the time of the return to Zion, Zerubbabel, a descendant of Jeconiah, appeared and led the people (an episode we shall discuss in the next chapter). But at that moment in history, Jeconiah's line was indeed cut off, and in his place Nebuchadnezzar installed Zedekiah, who ruled in Jerusalem until the destruction of the Temple in 586 BCE.

Jeremiah's prophecy about the future king called "YHWH is our righteousness" was made in the time of Zedekiah. Some commentators have therefore thought that this may have been an expression of messianic hopes for Zedekiah himself. But a different opinion among scholars, which I tend to accept, is that the wordplay with the name Zedekiah expressed criticism and despair of the king.

As in the case of Isaiah, I believe disappointment with the present king aroused Jeremiah's hopes for a messianic figure. Zedekiah was a weak king who often tried to maneuver his way between

Babylon and Egypt under pressure from his ministers. The prophet believed that this future role would not be held by Zedekiah, but by another king with an exalted name: *YHWH Zidkenu* (YHWH is our righteousness).

In 588 BCE, Zedekiah, unwisely relying on Egypt for military help, rebelled against the Babylonians. In response the Babylonians besieged Jerusalem, captured it, and burned down the Temple. The second book of Kings (25:1–7) tells us that Zedekiah tried to flee eastward in the direction of the Judean desert, but the Babylonians overtook him on the plains of Jericho and brought him before the Babylonian king to be judged. King Nebuchadnezzar passed a harsh sentence on Zedekiah. The Babylonians slaughtered his sons in front of him, blinded him, and took him to Babylon in chains. We do not know what happened to him after that.

Thus the city was destroyed, the Temple burned down, and broad sections of the people sent into exile. What is more, the Babylonians had cruelly humiliated the last, anointed king of the Davidic dynasty to rule in Judah, and it seemed that the end of the house of David had come. One may assume that many people in Jerusalem were deeply shocked by this turn of events. Zedekiah, after all, was perceived like all the other Davidic kings: as the anointed of God.

We find an expression of the people's distress in Psalm 89, which records the curses, contempt, and shame bestowed on Zedekiah:

> I have found David, my servant;
> with my holy oil I have anointed him;
> so that my hand shall ever abide with him,
> my arm also shall strengthen him.
> The enemy shall not outwit him,
> the wicked shall not humble him.
> I will crush his foes before him and strike
>   down those who hate him. . . .
> He shall cry to me,

"Thou art my Father, my God,
and the Rock of my salvation."
And I will make him the first-born,
the highest of the kings of the earth.
   (Ps. 89:20–23, 26–27)

The anointed king is called the first-born of God here, and the Davidic dynasty is promised perpetuity:

My steadfast love I will keep for him for ever,
and my covenant will stand firm for him.
I will establish his line for ever and his throne as
   the days of the heavens. (Ps. 89:28–29)

Next, the psalm expresses reservations concerning the king's successors:

If his children forsake my law and do not
   walk according to my ordinances,
if they violate my statutes and do not
   keep my commandments,
then I will punish their transgression with the
   rod and their iniquity with scourges;
but I will not remove from him my steadfast love,
or be false to my faithfulness.
I will not violate my covenant,
or alter the word that went forth from my lips.
Once for all I have sworn by my holiness;
I will not lie to David.
His line shall endure for ever,
his throne as long as the sun before me.
Like the moon it shall be established for ever;
it shall stand firm while the skies endure. (Ps. 89:30–37)

One of David's successors may sin and God will punish him, but the covenant with David and his house is eternal. Like the sun and moon, the throne of David will last forever.

Then the Psalmist addresses God in the second person to express his pain and frustration at the breaking of the divine promise and the divine covenant with David:

> But now thou hast cast off and rejected,
> thou art full of wrath against thy anointed.
> Thou hast renounced the covenant with thy servant,
> thou hast defiled his crown in the dust.
> Thou hast breached all his walls;
> thou hast laid his strongholds in ruins.
> All that pass despoil him;
> he has become the scorn of his neighbors. . . .
> Thou hast removed the scepter from his hand,
> and cast his throne to the ground.
> Thou hast cut short the days of his youth;
> thou hast covered him with shame. (Ps. 89:38–41, 44–45)

We can sense the shame and humiliation at the fate of Zedekiah. At last, the Psalmist concludes:

> Lord, where is thy steadfast love of old,
> which by thy faithfulness thou didst swear to David?
> Remember, O Lord, how thy servant is scorned;
> how I bear in my bosom the insults of the
>   peoples, with which thy enemies taunt,
> O Lord, with which they mock the footsteps
>   of thy anointed. (Ps. 89:49–51)

The expression "the footsteps of thy anointed" (which would later take the form of "the footsteps of the Messiah" and become a familiar expression in Jewish thought) refers to Zedekiah, the last anointed king of the Davidic dynasty. By "steadfast love" the psalmist is asking God to remember the divine promise to David.

Another such expression of the people's pain is found in the book of Lamentations, written in the period of the destruction of the First Temple. Jewish tradition has ascribed authorship of Lamentations to Jeremiah because he was the prophet active at the time of the destruction, but the books of Lamentations and Jeremiah are not at all similar in content or style, and so it is unreasonable to think Jeremiah was the author. Lamentations was written by an anonymous author of the generation of the destruction, and it seems that he too saw Zedekiah, king of Judah, as the anointed of God:

> Our pursuers were swifter than the
>   vultures in the heavens;
> they chased us on the mountains, they lay
>   in wait for us in the wilderness.
> The breath of our nostrils, the Lord's
>   anointed, was taken in their pits,
> he of whom we said,
> "Under his shadow we shall live among
>   the nations." (Lam. 4:19–20)

The hunt in the wilderness leads to the capture of Zedekiah, who is called "the breath of our nostrils, the Lord's anointed."

There is an interesting parallel to this expression in Egyptian literature, where the king is called "the breath of the nostrils" of his subjects—in other words, they cannot live without him; he provides them with their very existence. Here, too, the author is expressing a similar hope of some of the people—that of "living under the shadow" of the king—but this hope is dashed with Zedekiah's capture.

Jeremiah, who of course did not share these sentiments, was not exiled to Babylon like most of the population of Judah after the conquest of Jerusalem. He continued to prophesy in the Land of Israel for a short period of time, until other forces contrived to remove him from the land. The Babylonians had put Gedaliah, son of Ahikam, in charge of the Jews remaining in the country. But after a year or two, Ishmael, son of Nethaniah, murdered Gedaliah, and Ishmael's companions, fearing the Babylonians, fled to Egypt, taking Jeremiah with them against his will. For the next several years, Jeremiah continued to prophesy to this group of Jews, rebuking them for worshiping pagan idols in Egypt.

The Babylonian system of exile was different from the Assyrian method in a way that would prove significant for the history of the people of Israel. The Assyrian rulers, aiming to destroy the national identities of the peoples they conquered, changed the places of residence of whole peoples throughout the empire and imposed a uniform "one language and one speech" on a vast area. This led all those exiled to Assyria—including the ten tribes and the Judeans exiled from the area of Lachish during Sennacherib's campaign of 701 BCE—to disappear in the Assyrian melting pot. But the Assyrians did not succeed in conquering Jerusalem, which lasted another 115 years, until the Babylonian empire took control of the city and exiled its inhabitants. And, to the good fortune of the Jewish people, the Babylonians permitted every exiled group to continue to live together and maintain a kind of cultural and religious autonomy.

On the River Kvar in Babylonia there lived a Jewish community. One of its towns was called Tel-Aviv, and, Ezekiel's prophecies tell us, Tel-Aviv had an autonomous life from both national and religious points of view. Members of the community kept their Jewish names (as attested by quite a number of documents found in the area). The community did not perform sacrifices, on the grounds of the biblical conception that doing so outside the Land of Israel, in the "land of the peoples" where there was uncleanliness, was forbidden. In the famous psalm depicting the exiles weeping by the rivers of Babylon as they remember Zion, when those in charge are asked to sing, their answer, "How shall we sing the Lord's song in a foreign land?" (Ps. 137:4), was not only an expression of sadness and nostalgia, but a religious matter. As we see in the book of Chronicles, singing "the Lord's song" was a ritual act. The Bible forbade the Jews from performing all cultic activity in an impure foreign land.

In short, in Babylonia there was for the first time an important Jewish community, with Jewish life and a Jewish religious life, but without a temple, without an altar, and without sacrifices, for about fifty years. We do not know how the members of that community preserved their religious identity, but observance of the Sabbath seems to have been a matter of great importance to them. This is reflected in the prophecy of the second Isaiah (the anonymous prophet to whom some chapters of Isaiah are attributed), who lived in this period: "All who keep the sabbath and do not profane it / And who hold fast to My covenant—I will bring them to My sacred mount / And let them rejoice in My house of prayer" (Isa. 56:6–7). Perhaps the people found the observance of the Sabbath a replacement for the sanctity of the Temple. Some scholars think that the origins of the institution of the synagogue are to be found in this community in Babylon, although we have no solid evidence for this.

In 539 BCE, about forty-five years after the destruction of the Temple, King Cyrus of Persia conquered Babylon. The last king in Babylon before it was conquered was Nabonidus, a special and fascinating figure. Nabonidus was not of royal stock. Born to a priestess in the temple of the god Sin in the town of Haran (today in southwestern Turkey, not far from the Syrian border), he was an enthusiastic devotee of that god. At one point, Nabonidus attempted to impose the rites of the god Sin on the city of Babylon and on the main temple there, which was devoted to the god Marduk. The priests of the temple of Marduk were very angry with Nabonidus, and thus when Cyrus, king of Persia, reached

Babylon in 539 BCE, they opened the gates, Cyrus entered, and he conquered the city without a siege or battle.

In a cuneiform inscription on a clay cylinder that appears to have been written under the influence of the priests of Marduk, Cyrus is described as a righteous king chosen by Marduk to rule the world. It was as an emissary of Marduk that Cyrus conquered Babylon, renewed the former rituals, and restored the temples.

Interestingly, similar descriptions are found in the writings of the prophet known to scholars as the Second Isaiah, the anonymous author of chapters 40–55 of the book of Isaiah. I accept the opinion of the English scholar Hugh Williamson[1] that the Second Isaiah probably edited the prophecies of his predecessor, Isaiah, and added to these his own, which are largely commentaries on and interpretations of the prophecies of the First Isaiah.

There is a certain linguistic affinity and sense of continuity between the two prophets, but at the same time one should bear in mind the huge historical and geographical gaps between them. The first Isaiah, son of Amoz, lived in Jerusalem in the second half of the eighth century BCE, and the Second Isaiah was active in Babylon in the mid-sixth century BCE. Naturally, there are incongruities and differences between the two Isaiahs, and one of them concerns the main question we are dealing with—that of the Messiah.

In one of the prophecies of the Second Isaiah, we read:

Thus says the Lord, your Redeemer, who formed you from the womb: "I am the Lord, who made all things, who stretched out the heavens alone, who spread out the earth—Who was with me?—who frustrates the omens of liars, who turns wise men back, and makes their knowledge foolish; who confirms the word of his servant, and performs the counsel of his messengers; who says of Jerusalem, 'She shall be inhabited.' And of the cities of Judah, 'They shall be built, and I will raise up their ruins.'" (Isa. 44:24–26)

God tells the people not to trust the words of the wise and the omens of soothsayers, and conveys the message through his prophet that Jerusalem and the cities of Judah will be rebuilt. Verse 28 gives the context of this prophecy:

> Who says of Cyrus, "He is my shepherd, and he shall fulfill all my purpose"; saying of Jerusalem, "She shall be built," and of the temple, "Your foundation shall be laid."

Here Cyrus, king of Persia, is described as God's emissary who does God's will through his promise to build the Temple in Jerusalem.

Two versions of Cyrus's famous declaration in which this decision appears have come down to us: one in Hebrew and one in Aramaic.[2] The Hebrew version relates how the God of heaven sent Cyrus to restore the Temple in Jerusalem. Cyrus gave permission for all the implements of the Temple taken by the Babylonians to be returned to the Land of Israel and for the earlier sacrifices to be resumed there. The Persian king who restored the Babylonian rites of the god Marduk in Babylon thus also restored the rituals of the God of heaven in Jerusalem. In the eyes of the Second Isaiah, this earned Cyrus the title of shepherd ("Who says of Cyrus, 'He is my shepherd'") generally bestowed on the kings of the house of David (in 2 Samuel 5:2, for instance, or in Ezekiel 34:23).

The transfer of the title "shepherd" from kings of the house of David to a foreign king is surprising enough, but in the following verse we find an even more unexpected title:

> Thus says the Lord to his anointed, to Cyrus, whose right hand I have grasped, to subdue nations before him that gates may not be closed: I will go before you and level the mountains, I will break in pieces the doors of bronze and cut asunder the bars of iron, I will give you the treasures of darkness and the hoards in secret places, that you may know that it is I, the Lord, the God of Israel, who call you by your name. (Isa. 45:1–3)

God holds Cyrus's right hand, opens doors for him (perhaps this hints at the way he conquered Babylon), and calls him by his name, as we saw in the Babylonian inscription. But most surprising of all are the opening words: "Thus says the Lord to his anointed, to Cyrus": the traditional holy title connected with the sacred rite of anointing with oil is bestowed here on a foreign king!

This is quite extraordinary, and we have to ask: if Cyrus is a shepherd and anointed, what is left for the house of David? The prophet gives us the answer later on:

> Ho, every one who thirsts, come to the waters; and he who has no money, come, buy and eat! Come, buy wine and milk without money and without price. Why do you spend your money for that which is not bread, and your labor for that which does not satisfy? Hearken diligently to me and eat what is good, and delight yourselves in fatness. Incline your ear and come to me; hear, that your soul may live; and I will make with you an everlasting covenant, my steadfast, sure love for David. (Isa. 55:1–3)

Thus the Second Isaiah turned to the community in Babylon and declared that the covenant made with David was now transferred to them, to every one of them. The royal messianic figure from the house of David was replaced by Cyrus, and God now gave the promise of continuity and permanence bestowed on David and his successors to the entire people.

The prophet's audacious and surprising reversal here dispensed with the traditional messianic figure from the house of David. This was of course in total opposition to the view of the First Isaiah, who, with all his disappointment with the contemporary kings of the house of David, hoped for a future king who would sit on David's throne, "a shoot from the stump of Jesse" (see Isa. 9:6–7; 11:1).

In addition to Cyrus, the foreign Messiah, the Second Isaiah portrayed another figure to whom he devoted a number of prophecies: the "servant of the Lord." This servant is a mysterious and intriguing figure, especially on account of his sufferings and the fact that that this suffering is an atonement for others. Much ink has been spilled in an effort to determine who this suffering servant could be. The Christian church says that the suffering servant was Jesus. The sages suggested that he was Moses, who is called "Moses, my servant" in the Torah and who suffered so much from the people of Israel that in a moment of crisis he asked God to kill him in order to release him from the burden of leading them (Num. 11:11–15). This was also the opinion of the Austrian Bible scholar and archaeologist Ernst Sellin (1867–1946), who did not know the talmudic sources but thought that Moses was the suffering servant and that the children of Israel had killed him. His *Introduction to the Old Testament*, published in Vienna, reached the hands of Sigmund Freud, who went on to present in his famous work *Moses and Monotheism* that Moses was killed by the people of Israel.

To this day, the identity of the "suffering servant" remains an enigma. Commentators and scholars wonder whether he was an actual person from the past (Moses or one of the kings of Judah) or future (a Messiah or Jesus, as is professed in the New Testament), or whether he was a collective figure, representing the people of Israel or the righteous among the people of Israel. My own opinion is that of Ibn Ezra in his twelfth-century commentary on the book of Isaiah: the servant is sometimes a collective figure and sometimes a particular figure identified with the prophet himself.

A number of cases show that the term "my servant" refers to the whole people of Israel. For instance:

But you, Israel, my servant, Jacob, whom I have chosen,
   the offspring of Abraham, my friend; you whom I took
   from the ends of the earth, and called from its farthest
   corners, saying to you, "You are my servant, I have
   chosen you and not cast you off" (Isa. 41:8–9);

Remember these things, O Jacob, and Israel, for you are
   my servant (44:21);
For the sake of my servant Jacob, and Israel my chosen
   (45:4);
The Lord has redeemed his servant Jacob (48:20).

But other examples indicate that the servant is not the same as
the people of Israel. Thus, for example, at the beginning of chapter
49 there is a prophecy of a personal character:

Listen to me, O coastlands, and hearken, you peoples from
afar. The Lord called me from the womb, from the body of my
mother he named my name. He made my mouth like a sharp
sword, in the shadow of his hand he hid me. (Isa. 49:1–2)

This vocation from the womb is reminiscent of the beginning of
the book of Jeremiah:

Now the word of the Lord came to me saying, "Before I formed
you in the womb I knew you, and before you were born I
consecrated you; I appointed you a prophet to the nations."
(Jer. 1:4–5)

The succeeding verses in Isaiah also portray the servant as a personal figure:

And now the Lord says, who formed me from the womb to be
his servant, to bring Jacob back to him, and that Israel might
be gathered to him, for I am honored in the eyes of the Lord,
and my God has become my strength—he says: "It is too light
a thing that you should be my servant to raise up the tribes of
Jacob and to restore the preserved of Israel; I will give you as
a light to the nations, that my salvation may reach to the end
of the earth." (Isa. 49:5–6)

God had created him from the womb to be his servant, and he had the task of bringing Jacob—that is, the people of Israel—back to God. Yet God characterized this initial task as easy: "It is too light a thing that you should be my servant to raise up the tribes of Jacob and to restore the preserved of Israel" (49:6a). He is faced with another, more complex task: to bring light and salvation to all peoples: "I will give you as a light to the nations, that my salvation may reach to the end of the earth" (49:6b). If one of the servant's tasks is to bring Israel back to God, one cannot interpret the servant as being the people of Israel.

It would appear then that in these verses, the servant of God sent to the nations to bring salvation to the end of the earth is the prophet himself. In the prophecy in chapter 42, it says specifically that God gave the servant the divine spirit of prophecy:

Behold my servant, whom I uphold, my chosen, in whom my soul delights; I have put my spirit upon him, he will bring forth justice to the nations. (Isa. 42:1)

In the continuation of this prophecy, there is a very interesting description of the servant:

He will not cry or lift up his voice, or make it heard in the street; a bruised reed he will not break, and a dimly burning wick he will not quench; he will faithfully bring forth justice. He will not fail or be discouraged till he has established justice in the earth; and the coastlands wait for his law. (42:2–3)

This is a paradoxical figure. On the one hand, the servant is weak and wretched: he cannot cry out or break a bruised reed; he doesn't even have the strength to put out a wick that is scarcely burning. Yet despite his physical weakness, he can "establish justice in the earth," and distant coastlands wait for his law.

His mission to the nations reappears a little further on:

I am the Lord, I have called you in righteousness, I have taken you by the hand and kept you; I have given you as a covenant to the people, a light to the nations, to open the eyes that are blind, to bring out the prisoners from the dungeon, from the prison those who sit in darkness. I am the Lord, that is my name; my glory I give to no other, nor my praise to graven images. (Isa. 42:6–8)

It seems that here, again, the words refer to the prophet sent to be "a light to the nations." The nations of the world in their blindness worship idols. The servant is sent to them to open their eyes and teach them the truth about God: "I am the Lord, that is my name; my glory I give to no other, nor my praise to graven images."

This description of the servant as someone who will teach the nations and establish justice on earth recalls the first Isaiah's prophecy:

It shall come to pass in the latter days that the mountain of the house of the Lord shall be established as the highest of the mountains, and shall be raised above the hills; and all the nations shall flow to it, and many peoples shall come and say: "Come, let us go up to the mountain of the Lord, to the house of the God of Jacob; that he may teach us his ways and that we may walk in his paths." For out of Zion shall go forth the law, and the word of the Lord from Jerusalem. He shall judge between the nations, and shall decide for many peoples; and they shall beat their swords into plowshares, and their spears into pruning hooks; nation shall not lift up sword against nation, neither shall they learn war any more. (Isa. 2:2–4)

And yet the very tasks the First Isaiah ascribes to God—teaching the nations and judging between them—the Second Isaiah now bestows upon the servant.

Once again, we see the elevation of the figure of the servant and his spiritual powers—to the point that God's functions are represented here as his own. At the same time, the servant's bodily weakness is one of his defining characteristics. In his weakness he is the opposite of a strong, heroic king or the future figure described by the First Isaiah as "Mighty God." The servant is anything but mighty.

Later in the same chapter, the Second Isaiah says: "The Lord goes forth like a mighty man, like a man of war he stirs up his fury; he cries out, he shouts aloud, he shows himself mighty against his foes" (Isa. 42:13). In other words, there is power, but in the spirit of the "Song of the Sea" ("The Lord is a man of war; the Lord is his name," Exod. 15:3), it is ascribed to God.

This difference in the character of the messianic figure is of course connected to the great difference in the historical situations in which the texts were written. The earliest parts of the book of Isaiah echo the psalms of praise written in the classical period of the monarchy. In those days, there were two strong kingdoms ruled by warrior-kings who gave their peoples military and territorial victories. The title "Messiah" (anointed) was given to a king sitting on his throne (for instance, in Psalm 45 and Psalm 2). As we have seen, the expansion of Assyria in the eighth century BCE brought the kingdom of Israel to an end and greatly weakened the kingdom of Judah. This gave rise to the hope of Isaiah, followed by Jeremiah, for a figure—the "Mighty God," or "YHWH is our righteousness"—who would replace the weak and disappointing kings of their times. But although both prophets described that figure as "mighty," they were very suspicious and critical of dependence on human military strength, whether Jewish or foreign.

Cyrus's declaration totally changed the geopolitical map of the region. After two great empires that had effectuated the disappearance of the kingdom of Israel and the degradation and defeat of the kingdom of Judah, there suddenly appeared a new power whose totally different policy allowed the Judean exiles to return to their country and restore their Temple. The Second Isaiah saw that period as a time of redemption actualized by means of Cyrus, the king-Messiah. The king-Messiah was now no longer a future figure, but a real-life personage of the present day.

In this respect, after the disappearance of Assyria and Babylon, messianism reemerged as a contemporary view, but with notable differences. The title "Messiah" was taken from the house of David and given to a foreign king, Cyrus. Both the "promise to David" and the covenant made with the royal line were transferred to the people as a whole. And, at the same time, a new figure appeared: the suffering servant. He was physically weak—far from a hero of war—yet strong in his spirit and teaching.

Still, there is even more to be said about the last part of the book of Isaiah: chapters 56 to 66. The prophecies in these chapters were probably the product of yet another prophet: the third Isaiah, as scholars generally call him. He appears to have lived slightly after the time of Cyrus, although this prophet never mentions the Persian king. Nor does he ever speak of the figure of the servant central to the Second Isaiah.

At the same time, in one of his prophecies the verb for "anoint" (*mashiach*) is given a new and interesting application:

> The spirit of the Lord God is upon me, because the Lord has anointed me to bring good tidings to the afflicted: he has sent me to bind up the brokenhearted, to proclaim liberty to the captives, and the opening of the prison to those who are bound; to proclaim the year of the Lord's favor, and the day of vengeance of our God: to comfort all who mourn; to grant to those who mourn in Zion—to give them a garland instead of ashes, the oil of gladness instead of mourning, the mantle of praise instead of a faint spirit; that they may be called oaks of righteousness, the planting of the Lord that he may be glorified. (Isa. 61:1–3)

The speaker declares that God has anointed him and the spirit of the Lord is upon him. He is a kind of "Messiah of the spirit" (to use a term used by the writers of the Qumran sect).

It seems that here again, the prophet is speaking of himself. He sees himself as anointed with the spirit of the Lord and as a messenger bringing liberty and comfort to prisoners and mourners. The mourners are of course mourners of Zion, and the term *dror* (liberty) is parallel to the Babylonian term *andorerum,* which means a royal decree liberating all those enslaved for economic reasons. In fact, the prophet takes upon himself the royal-messianic task of proclaiming freedom in the land.

The Third Isaiah never mentions David or the house of David, and, as with the Second Isaiah, he replaces the expectation of a future revival of the rule of the house of David with a present-day anointing—in this case, of the prophet himself. And there is a further development, even more distant from the classical conception of a Messiah from the house of David, and connected with the continuous transformation of the term "to anoint." The anointing is no longer a physical anointing with oil, but a spiritual one: an anointing with the spirit of the Lord. As such, a "Messiah" is someone who possesses—that is, has been anointed with—the spirit of prophecy.

Thus it is that anointing gradually lost the concrete, material meaning it once had. Now and during all the period of the second Temple, including the time of the birth of Christianity, the name "Messiah" became detached from the actual act of pouring olive oil, but rather gained a spiritual meaning, and one relating to prophecy. In the eyes of the first Christians, the "Suffering Servant" prophecy was fulfilled in the figure of the suffering Jesus.

However, in the same period, others could not accept the Christian view about a semidivine Messiah. Like the student of Jeremiah who composed Jeremiah 33:14–16, they rejected the elevation of the Messiah to divine status.

4

Messianic Rise and Fall of "the Branch"

Among the Jewish exiles who left Babylon after King Cyrus of Persia gave the edict sanctioning their return to Jerusalem and the Temple's restoration were three prophets: Haggai, Zechariah, and Malachi. In their prophecies, the messianic idea continued to be developed.

Cyrus gave back to the Jews the utensils of the Temple taken by the Babylonians. The Persian king also declared that he would provide everything they needed for the renewal of the sacrifices. His only request was that when the Temple services were renewed, they would include a prayer for the king.

Cyrus's edict was very detailed, as we see in chapters 5 and 6 of the book of Ezra. In the time of King Darius, who inherited the kingdom after Cyrus's son Cambyses, some questions arose with regard to the building of the Temple in Jerusalem, and when Darius asked that the evidence of Cyrus's edict be searched for in the royal archives in the city of Achmata (summer capital of the kings of Persia and Media in northwestern Iran, today the Iranian city of Hamadan), the document found there specified the precise measurements of the proposed Temple, the materials to be used in its construction, and so on.

In contrast to the exactitude of these specifications, Cyrus's edict did not stipulate any rebuilding of the city of Jerusalem and its walls destroyed by the Babylonians. It would seem that his main interest was in religious-ceremonial matters, and so the restoration of the city as a whole did not concern him.

In fact, one may assume that the opposite was true. From Cyrus's point of view, it was best to leave the city open and unwalled. If the Jews in Jerusalem wanted to rebel or demand political independence, the state of the walls would make it very difficult for them. Indeed, when in a later period Nehemiah began to rebuild and restore the city walls, his enemies Sanballat the Horonite and Geshem the Arab accused him of fortifying the city in order to rebel against the Persian empire and declare himself king: "You and the Jews intend to rebel; that is why you are building the wall, and you wish to become their king, it is reported" (Neh. 6:6). We have no evidence, however, that these were Nehemiah's true intentions.

Thus the Persian kingdom supported the Jews' religious-ceremonial aspirations to restore the Temple and revive its rituals, while opposing the political and military restoration of Judah and Jerusalem. It was in this situation that there came into prominence a new figure among those who had returned to Zion and were active in the Temple's restoration: the High Priest.

In the Torah, the High Priest is called Messiah (anointed), as he, like the king, is anointed with oil: "If it is the anointed priest who sins, thus bringing guilt on the people" (Lev. 4:3). In the book of Exodus, a command to anoint the High Priest appears after a description of his splendid garments, including a diadem, a gold plate on his head, inscribed with the words "Holy to the Lord" (Exod. 28:36): "And you shall take the anointing oil, and pour it on his head and anoint him" (29:7).

The biblical scholar Julius Wellhausen and others who followed him claimed that this text was an innovation made in Second Temple times, because in that period, when the people of Israel no longer had a monarchy, the High Priest took the place of the king, and that was the background to the ritual of his anointing. However, we know today that like the anointing of kings, the anointing of priests was a pre-Israelite custom. This is supported by the interesting archive at Emar, close to the River Euphrates, which was expanded in the transition between the Bronze Age and the Iron Age in about the beginning of the twelfth century

BCE. One document from Emar describes the ceremonies for the installation of a priestess of the god Baal. Part of these rituals is the anointing of the intended priestess with oil.[1] As we saw in chapter 1, anointing is an enhancement, a bestowal of the splendor of sanctity, represented by the shining oil.

Thus the anointing of priests goes back to very ancient times, and there is no reason to think that the custom began in Israel only in the Second Temple period. Priests appear to have been already anointed in the First Temple period, and perhaps even earlier, in the time of the judges. Although we do not have specific evidence of anointing priests in the early monarchic period, we have much biblical evidence of the priests' great involvement in the political life of that period. Thus, for instance, we read of priests in the royal court, priests who went to war bearing the Ark of the Covenant, and priests carrying the Ummim and Thummim (elements connected with divination), on whom kings—Saul, and then David—relied.[2]

The last time we read about priests going forth with the Ark of the Covenant was during Absalom's revolt against David (2 Sam. 15:24). After that, prophets replaced them as counselors in time of war. For instance, the prophet Elisha advised King Yoram of Israel and King Jehoshaphat of Judah in their war against Moab, and the prophet Micaiah, son of Yimlah, told King Ahab of Israel how his war against Syria would transpire (2 Kings 3:15–19; 1 Kings 22:6–10). Thus the involvement of priests in wars and political affairs came to an end in the time of David. After Solomon built the Temple, the priests were confined to it. They were no longer involved in political and military spheres.

This division of spheres between the king, who led the people in wars and political matters, and the High Priest, ensconced in the Temple and concerned with ritual matters, continued throughout the time of the monarchy. The division then broke down in the time of the return to Zion. The Persian authorities did not allow the monarchy to be restored, and parallel with this, there was a rise in the political status of the priesthood. A similar change may be found in the words of the second Isaiah read in the last chapter: the prophet transferred the promises given to the house of David to the people as a whole and called Cyrus a "Messiah."

But it seems that the returnees to Zion who lived in Jerusalem were not convinced by the second Isaiah's prophesy. They wished to retain their allegiance to the house of David and hoped that a ruler of his line would still arise to govern the community. And among the first of those to return there was such a person: Zerubbabel ben Shealtiel, apparently the grandson of King Jeconiah.

The prophets Haggai and Zechariah, each in his own way, placed great hopes in Zerubbabel. Zechariah refers frequently to the dual leadership of the returnees to Zion: that of the High Priest, a dignitary of the Persian monarchy, who naturally held a high position; and that of Zerubbabel, a dignitary among the people and a descendant of the royal line. A question that often arose in the prophecies of the period was whether these two leaders could rule together.

In a famous vision, Zechariah saw a golden lampstand with seven lamps and two olive trees beside them. When the prophet asked the meaning of this apparition, at first he did not receive an answer:

> And I said to the angel who talked with me, "What are these, my lord?" Then the angel who talked with me answered me, "Do you not know what these are?" I said, "No, my lord." (Zech. 4:4–5)

Then the angel gave him a message for Zerubbabel:

> Then he said to me, "This is the word of the Lord to Zerubbabel: Not by might, nor by power, but by my Spirit, says the Lord of hosts." (Zech. 4:6)

That is to say, success would not be achieved through political or military power. Deliverance could only come from the spirit of God.

But Zechariah was not finished with his questioning. He persisted, asking two more questions:

> Then I said to him, "What are these two olive trees on the right and the left of the lampstand?" And a second time I said to him, "What are these two branches of the olive trees, which are beside the two golden pipes from which the oil is poured out?" (4:11–12)

Then the angel finally satisfied his curiosity, answering:

> "These are the two sons of Yitzhar who stand by the Lord of the whole earth." (4:14)

The two olive branches to the left and right of the lampstand were the "sons of Yitzhar"—that is to say, the sons of olive oil. These two figures anointed with oil "stood by the Lord of the whole earth" as servants of God and members of the heavenly host (the angels).

One may deduce that in Zechariah's vision there was an aggrandizement of the anointed (messianic) figures of the period: the ruler from the house of David, Zerubbabel ben Shealtiel, and the High Priest, Joshua ben Jehozadak. Both of them stood before God as anointed emissaries.

We also find an aggrandizement of the High Priest in other prophecies of Zechariah:

> Then he showed me Joshua the high priest standing before the angel of the Lord, and Satan standing at his right hand to accuse him. And the Lord said to Satan, "The Lord rebuke you, O Satan! The Lord who has chosen Jerusalem rebuke you! Is this not a brand plucked from the fire?" Now Joshua was standing before the angel, clothed with filthy garments. And the angel said

to those standing before him, "Remove the filthy garments from him." And to him he said, "Behold, I have taken your iniquity away from you, and I will clothe you with rich apparel." And I said, "Let them put a clean turban on his head." So they put a clean turban on his head and clothed him with garments; and the angel of the Lord was standing by. And the angel of the Lord enjoined Joshua, "Thus says the Lord of hosts: If you walk in my ways and keep my charge, then you shall rule my house and have charge of my courts, and I will give you the right of access among those who are standing here." (Zech. 3:1–7)

It is hard to know exactly what the filthy garments signified: or, that is to say, what Joshua's defilement was. Was it a symbol of the people's sin, which the priest bore on his shoulders in accordance with the priestly concept that the priest bears the sin of the community (e.g., in Lev. 10:17, "that you may bear the iniquity of the congregation")? Or could it have been, as Yehezkel Kaufmann thought,[3] the existential impurity a man feels when standing before God? This last suggestion is somewhat reminiscent of Isaiah's cry amid his vision of the heavenly throne, "Woe is me! For I am lost; for I am a man of unclean lips" (Isa. 6:5). In both cases, there is a kind of ceremony to cleanse the impurity. In Isaiah's vision, a seraph takes a burning coal from the altar and touches the lips of the prophet with it, and in that way makes him fit to appear among the angels and receive a prophetic mission. In Zechariah's vision the dressing with clean clothes enables the priest to join the heavenly host: "and I will give you the right of access among those who are standing here."

Whatever the case, in the continuation of Zechariah's vision there is an important figure called "the Branch," whose arrival God announces to the High Priest:

"Hear, now, O Joshua the high priest, you and your friends who sit before you, for they are men of good omen: behold, I will bring my servant the Branch." (Zech. 3:8).

Who is this mysterious Branch? This term occurs once again in a prophecy in which Zechariah proclaims:

> Thus says the Lord of hosts, "Take from them silver and gold, and make a crown, and set it upon the head of Joshua, the son of Jehozadak, the high priest, and say to him, 'Thus says the Lord of hosts, Behold the man whose name is the Branch: for he shall grow up in his place, and he shall build the temple of the Lord, and shall bear royal honor, and shall sit and rule upon his throne. And there shall be a priest by his throne, and peaceful understanding shall be between them both.'" (Zech. 6:11–13).

Thus, on the one hand, the high priest Joshua ben Jehozadak is given a crown of silver and gold. On the other hand, another figure called "the Branch" is to build the temple of the Lord and sit on a throne and rule—though next to him will be another throne for the priest. The prophet's hope that there will be "peaceful understanding between them"—between the priest and the Branch—suggests that in practice, relations between these two officeholders were not so peaceful.

Commentators and scholars disagree about the identity of this Branch. Some hold that it was a code name for Zerubbabel ben Shealtiel. Others believe it was someone else who would replace Zerubbabel after his surprising disappearance from the biblical scene (which we will discuss later). I tend to favor the first explanation. It seems to me that Zerubbabel was called "the Branch" in view of verses in the book of Jeremiah (discussed further in the last chapter):

> Behold, the days are coming, says the Lord, when I will raise up for David a righteous Branch, and he shall reign as king and deal wisely, and shall execute justice and righteousness in the land. In his days Judah will be saved, and Israel will dwell securely. And this is the name by which he will be called: "The Lord our righteousness." (Jer. 23:5–6)

It would seem that Zechariah latched onto the messianic hopes of his predecessor Jeremiah for a future king of the house of David, a "righteous Branch," and attached them to Zerubbabel, a descendant of the royal line. Perhaps a semantic resemblance can also be found here between the word *tzemach* ("branch") and the name Zerubbabel ("seed of Babylon"), both of which belong to the sphere of vegetation.

If Zerubbabel is intended, Zechariah's words, "Behold, I will bring my servant the Branch" can be understood as follows: *The hoped-for redeemer is in fact here, and he is Zerubbabel, a descendant of the house of David. Although Zerubbabel is now an official of the Persian kingdom, he will very soon become a "Branch," sit on the royal throne of the house of David, restore the former splendor, and save Judah.*

At the time, an open expression of messianic aspiration of this kind was liable to be disastrous. Enemies abounded who sought to report to the Persian authorities the slightest sign of the people's disloyalty to the king. Moreover, the Persian empire would send agents to the various peoples throughout the kingdom to detect signs of rebellion and deal with them. Scholars have suggested that the figure of Satan, the accuser of the High Priest Joshua ben Jehozadak in Zechariah's earlier vision, was based on an official of this kind who went around the country on the authorities' behalf. This would appear to be the reason why Zechariah used a code name, "Branch," and did not openly speak of Zerubbabel and the messianic hopes he placed in him.

Likewise, in the declarations of the prophet Haggai, who was active in the same period, we find similar messianic expectations. In one prophecy Haggai sought to convince the people and their two leaders, Zerubbabel and Joshua the priest, that even though the Temple being built now was wretched in comparison with the original Temple that had been destroyed, in the future there would be a dramatic change:

For thus says the Lord of hosts: "Once again, in a little while, I will shake the heavens and the earth and the sea and the dry land; and I will shake all nations, so that the treasures of all nations shall come in, and I will fill this house with splendor," says the Lord of hosts. "The silver is mine, and the gold is mine," says the Lord of hosts. "The latter splendor of the house shall be greater than the former," says the Lord of hosts; "and in this place I will give prosperity," says the Lord of hosts. (Hag. 2:6–9)

This prophecy was made around the year 520 BCE, in the second year of the reign of King Darius, a difficult year for the Persian empire. As a result of the wars of succession between Darius and a claimant to the throne who maintained he was a son of Cyrus, there were rebellions in several provinces in the empire, and especially in Babylon. Haggai, influenced by these events, predicted that God would shake the heavens and the earth and the nations of the world, and "the treasures of all nations" would come to Jerusalem. Thus the glory of the present Temple would be greater than that of the first one.

Haggai also predicted great things for Zerubbabel. In order to understand the verses we are about to read, keep in mind that Zerubbabel appears to have been the grandson of Jeconiah, concerning whom Jeremiah had predicted there would be no continuation of his line:

O land, land, land, hear the word of the Lord! Thus says the Lord: "Write this man down as childless, a man who shall not succeed in his days; for none of his offspring shall succeed in sitting on the throne of David, and ruling again in Judah." (Jer. 22:29–30)

Jeremiah compared Jeconiah to a signet ring on the right hand of God which the Divine tears off and throws to the ground:

As I live, says the Lord, though Jeconiah the son of Jehoiakim, king of Judah, were like a signet ring on my right hand, yet I would tear you off. (Jer. 22:24)

But the prophet Haggai disagreed with Jeremiah about the continuation of the line of David, and argued with him. He used this same image of a signet ring on God's hand, but turned Jeremiah's statement on its head:

On the twenty-fourth day of the ninth month, in the second year of Darius [520 BCE] the word of the LORD came by Haggai the prophet. . . . The word of the Lord came a second time to Haggai on the twenty-fourth day of the month, Speak to Zerubbabel, governor of Judah, saying, I am about to shake the heavens and the earth, and to overthrow the throne of kingdoms; I am about to destroy the strength of the kingdoms of the nations, and overthrow the chariots and their riders; and the horses and their riders shall go down, everyone by the sword of his fellow. On that day, says the Lord of hosts, I will take you, O Zerubbabel my servant, the son of Shealtiel, says the Lord, and make you like a signet ring; for I have chosen you, says the Lord of hosts. (Hag. 2:10, 20–23)

In view of the turmoil in the empire, Haggai expected an all-out war in which the kingdoms of the nations would destroy one another and the fighters would slay one another with swords. Then God would take hold of Zerubbabel, son of Shealtiel, and place him as a signet ring on his hand. The meaning was clear: Persia would be destroyed together with its enemies, and the one crowned as ruler would be Zerubbabel, the king from the house of David.

Thus we see that in the time of Zerubbabel, factions of the people had strong messianic hopes and expected deliverance to be near at hand.

Against this background, the question arose of the fasts for commemorating the destruction of the Temple, a question emerging among the messianic movements in Judaism from that time up until today. If the Messiah is coming soon and redemption is at hand, does one have to continue to observe the fasts for the destruction of the Temple? ("'Should I mourn and fast in the fifth month, as I have done for so many years?'" [Zech. 7:3]).

At first, Zechariah ignored the question, and like other prophets stressed the importance of behaving in a moral manner rather than fasting:

> Then the word of the Lord of hosts came to me; "Say to all the people of the land and the priests, when you fasted and mourned in the fifth month and in the seventh, for these seventy years, was it for me that you fasted? And when you eat and when you drink, do you not eat for yourselves and drink for yourselves?" . . . Thus says the Lord of hosts, Render true judgment, show kindness and mercy each to his brother. Do not oppress the widow, the fatherless, the sojourner, or the poor, and let none of you devise evil against his brother in your heart. (Zech. 7:4–6,9–10)

But, further on Zechariah said specifically:

> Thus says the Lord of hosts; Behold, I will save my people from the east country and from the west country; and I will bring them to dwell in the midst of Jerusalem; and they shall be my people and I will be their God, in faithfulness and in righteousness. . . . Thus says the Lord of hosts: the fast of the fourth month, and the fast of the fifth, and the fast of the seventh, and the fast of the tenth, shall be to the house of Judah seasons of joy and gladness, and cheerful feasts; therefore love, truth and peace. (8:7–8,18–19)

That is to say, the four fasts in Judaism in memory of the destruction of Jerusalem and the Temple—the fasts of the seventeenth of

Tammuz, the ninth of Av, the third of Tishre (fast of Gedaliah), and the tenth of Tevet—were to be canceled and become days of rejoicing. The returnees to Zion felt that the days of the Messiah were approaching—and together with them, the ingathering of the exiles, the completion of the Second Temple, and the renewal of the kingdom of the house of David.

The question about the fast was raised in 516 BCE, the fourth year of King Darius (Zech. 7:1). And in 515 BCE, only about a year after this prophecy was made, the building of the Second Temple was completed, but surprisingly Zerubbabel does not appear in the description of the dedication of the Temple in the book of Ezra (Ezra 6:14–18). The passage mentions the names of Haggai and Zechariah, but Zerubbabel is missing—and he is never again mentioned in the Bible. In other words, in the few short years between 520, when Haggai prophesied that "the latter splendor of the house shall be greater than the former" and that the Lord "will take you, O Zerubbabel my servant, the son of Shealtiel . . . and make you like a signet ring; for I have chosen you"—that the kingdom of the house of David would be renewed and Zerubbabel crowned as king—and 515 BCE, when the Second Temple was completed, the leader behind the building of the Temple disappeared, and we have no idea where to and for what reason.

Did Zerubbabel die a natural death? Or did the Persians hear rumors of the messianic hopes that he would renew the rule of the Davidic kingdom—their suspicions necessitating the covert reference to him as "the Branch"—and kill him or send him into exile in a distant province? Could they have taken him to one of the royal cities in Persia to keep him under surveillance? We do not know; all these are possibilities.

As soon as Zerubbabel left the biblical scene, hopes for a Messiah of the house of David fell into a slumber lasting four hundred years. Only in about the year 100 BCE, among the Qumran sect, would the expectation of a Messiah of the house of David be revived.

The messianic vacuum left by Zerubbabel was filled by aspirations of another kind. Great hopes were now placed in the second pillar of leadership at this time: the High Priest.

In the book of Malachi, the third of the prophets of the period, there is no mention of Zerubbabel or any other figure of the house of David. Malachi, who was active slightly later than Haggai and Zechariah, after the Temple was already built, dealt at length with matters pertaining to the Temple and priesthood. In one of his prophecies, he depicted the ideal figure of a priest:

> So shall you know that I have sent this command to you, that my covenant with Levi may hold, says the Lord of hosts. My covenant with him was a covenant of life and peace, and I gave them to him, that he might fear; and he feared me, he stood in awe of my name. True Torah was in his mouth, and no wrong was found on his lips. He walked with me in peace and upright-ness, and he turned many from iniquity. For the lips of a priest should guard knowledge, and men should seek Torah from his mouth, for he is the angel of the Lord of hosts. (Mal. 2:4–7)

We have already seen the analogy of a priest to an angel in Zechariah's vision concerning the High Priest Joshua ben Jehoza-dak, "And I will give you the right of access among those who are standing here" (Zech. 3:7), but here we no longer have a descrip-tion of the "two sons of Yitzhar"—that is, the dual leadership of the priest and the descendant of the house of David—but the sole leadership of the priest.

Here we must again bear in mind the historical situation. Unlike its predecessors, who were hostile to the Temple and its ritual, the Persian empire encouraged the people of Israel to return to their land, rebuild the Temple, and renew the Temple sacrifices. On the other hand, the Persian authorities did not tolerate mani-festations of political independence by any peoples. This gave rise to an indecisiveness among the returnees to Zion. Should they be content with what the Persian kingdom offered in the ceremonial realm, or should they revolt and appoint a new king of the house of David? One may assume that certain groups in Jerusalem in the time of the return to Zion wanted to appoint Zerubbabel or someone else as king, but it seems that the main priestly leadership decided differently. *Let us forget all hopes for a Messiah of the house of David*, they thought, *and from now on the High Priest in the Temple will be the leader of the people.*

Another interesting detail is to be found in the verses we have read from the book of Malachi. Twice in the sayings of the prophet an association is made between a priest and Torah (instruction): "True Torah was in his mouth" and "for the lips of a priest should guard knowledge and men should seek Torah from his mouth" (Mal. 2:6–7). The custom or the recommendation to turn to the priests in matters of Torah, generally in a ritual context, is known to us from other prophets, such as Haggai ("Thus said the Lord of Hosts: seek a ruling [Torah] from the priests," Hag. 2:11), but here there is a special emphasis on the relationship between those learned in Torah and the instruction of the people. Perhaps this should be seen in relation to one of the outstanding figures of the period: the priest Ezra, who was active in Jerusalem and instructed the people of Israel in Torah. The sages even ascribed the book of Malachi to him, although there is no real proof of that.

Do Malachi's words refer obliquely to the historical figure of Ezra and his work in editing the Torah and bringing it to the people? With this we shall begin the next chapter. Meanwhile, the tension between the High Priest and the royal messianic leader Zerubbabel in this generation would reappear later in a different form—in the trial of Jesus before the High Priest.

5

Shifting Sands of Torah Authority

In 459 BCE, Ezra the Scribe arrived in the Land of Israel. He belonged to a later wave of immigration than that of Zerubbabel and the High Priest Joshua (who had arrived in 538 BCE), for despite King Cyrus's declaration and the Persian authorities' encouragement of the Jews' return from Babylon, the Jews had responded to the call only partially. From various documents in our possession we know that the Jewish community in Babylon engaged in agriculture and trade, and not all Jews were eager to abandon their property and make the long journey to Jerusalem, a city in ruins, whose economic situation was not bright, and around which foreigners and enemies lay in wait.

Ezra was the leader of the second major wave of immigration. Chapter 8 of the book of Ezra lists all the Jews who came at that time, including Ezra, described as "a scribe (*sofer*) skilled in the law of Moses which the Lord God of Israel had given" (Ezra 7:6). This is the first time the title *scribe skilled in the law* appears in the Bible, and it seems to indicate the existence of a profession or group of "scribes of God's law." The title was not only a term of praise, acknowledging him as very learned, but reflected the tasks that Ezra had taken upon himself:

For Ezra had set his heart to study (*lidrosh*) the law of the Lord, and to do it, and to teach his statutes and ordinances in Israel. (Ezra 7:10)

Ezra, we learn, was a teacher who taught statutes and ordinances in Israel:

Artaxerxes, king of kings, to Ezra the priest, the scribe of the law of the God in heaven. And now I make a decree that any one of the people of Israel or their Priests or Levites in my kingdom, who freely offers to go to Jerusalem, may go with you. . . . And you, Ezra, according to the wisdom of your God which is in your hand, appoint magistrates and judges who may judge all the people in the province. Beyond the River, all such as know the laws of your God; and those who do not know them, you shall teach. (Ezra 7:12–13,25)

Artaxerxes I, who ruled over the Persian empire between 465 and 424 BCE, commanded Ezra to appoint magistrates and judges and to teach those who did not know the religious laws. In fact, the king gave Ezra the authority to impose the laws of the Torah on the members of his people, and even specified the punishments in store for transgressors:

Whoever will not obey the law of your God and the law of the king, let judgment be strictly executed upon him, whether for death or for banishment or for confiscation of his goods or for imprisonment. (Ezra 7:26)

Clearly, the figure of Ezra and the tasks he fulfilled were innovations. On the one hand, Ezra belonged to the line of priests who taught the law (*Torah*), as depicted, for instance, in the book of Haggai: "Seek ruling (*Torah*) from the priests" (Hag. 2:11). But *Torah* in this case was deciding on a certain law concerning matters of cleanliness and uncleanliness, whereas in the period of Ezra, *Torah* meant the totality of the laws in the Five Books of Moses. Although the scribes were connected to the priesthood, they included sages who functioned outside the circles of the Temple and the priesthood, people who specialized in knowledge of the Torah and who led the people on the strength of this erudition.

This was the beginning of a shift in the center of gravity from the former centers—the king's court, the Temple, the priesthood—to a new leadership connected with the law and the teaching of the law. Starting in the period of Ezra, who was active after Haggai and Zechariah and close to the time of Malachi, this process of transformation would continue into the eve of the destruction of the Temple (with figures such as Rabbi Yohanan ben Zakkai) and include, finally, the sages.

Ezra engaged in propagating the Torah, which was not known in Jerusalem in the edited form in which we know it today. As we saw, the book of Deuteronomy originated in the Northern Kingdom; only later, after the fall of Samaria, would it reach Jerusalem, where it would be edited and disseminated in Judah in the period of Josiah, around 620 BCE. But other texts than Deuteronomy were sources for the laws and stories of the Torah among the people of Israel, and before Ezra's time they had not yet become canonical.

The nature of these Torah materials, which may be divided into four main sources, is a very controversial matter that we will not enter into here. We can say this: at around 470 BCE there was a feeling that these sources needed to be edited and combined. An anonymous group of people in Babylon, whose identities are unknown to us, edited the four sources and worked them into a comprehensive whole; they constitute what we know today as the first four books of the Torah: Genesis, Exodus, Leviticus, and Numbers. To this unit the editors attached the book of Deuteronomy, which they already had in their possession since it had been published in the time of King Josiah before the exile. This is how the basic form of the five books of the Torah known to us today came into being.

In an earlier study, I suggested that the group responsible for this work of editing and rewriting belonged to a priestly popular school—that is to say, to priestly circles that were also open to more popular influence.[1] Part of the work of this group, which

I called "The Holiness School," was to combine the priestly and nonpriestly sources into a single narrative.

It thus seems that when Ezra came from Babylon, he brought with him the edited Torah, which was then unknown in the Land of Israel. Although the book of Deuteronomy was known in Jerusalem, besides the book of Deuteronomy the whole Torah assembled from various sources was not. That is why, on the first day of the seventh month, on the date known today as Rosh Hashanah (the New Year), there was a public ceremony to launch the new Torah:

> And all the people gathered as one man into the square before the Water Gate; and they told Ezra the scribe to bring the book of the law of Moses which the Lord had given to Israel. And Ezra the priest brought the law before the assembly, both men and women and all who could hear with understanding, on the first day of the seventh month. And he read from it facing the square before the Water Gate. (Neh. 8:1–3)

As we know, the Torah is not a short text, and Ezra read it out "from early morning until midday" (Neh. 8:3). The event was ceremonious: a wooden pulpit was made for Ezra to read the Torah, and when he opened the Book of the Torah, the whole people stood up. Ezra blessed God, the people stood while the Torah was read, and the Levites "helped the people to understand the law" (8:7). Between the rows stood Levites who already knew the texts, and explained them to the people. This, in fact, was the beginning of the process of interpreting the Torah, of the creation of an oral law explaining the written Torah:

> And they read from the book, from the law of God, clearly; and they gave the sense, so that the people understood the reading. (8:8)

The text relates that some of the people who heard the Torah wept, hearing for the first time laws they did not know and did not observe. Ezra comforted them and told them to go and eat and drink, "for the joy of the Lord is your strength" (8:10). The account makes clear the novelty of the new Torah for the people in Jerusalem, who were unaware of the process of editing that had taken place in Babylon. Thus we learn from the narrative that after the reading ceremony, the people celebrated the Feast of Tabernacles, with which they were unacquainted until that moment (see Neh. 8:13–17). The ceremony to launch the Torah marked the beginning of the educational process of learning and applying the new texts.

This was the beginning of a process in which the study and teaching of Torah was transferred from the "professional" groups, the priests and judges, to the class of scribes and sages, with whose help all of the people were now being invited to read and understand it. Now, for the first time, a farmer or a carpenter from a small village could become a spiritual leader, due to his great ability in learning and teaching Torah. The poor shepherd Akiva became the leading scholar of his generation (around 110–35 CE).

The ramifications of the partial democratization of learning and teaching Torah would be seen full-blown in the time of Jesus. Both the Pharisees and Jesus belonged to this new group of popular teachers who clashed with the old and elitist class of leaders, the priesthood.

6

Torah Distinctions between the Human and the Divine

Deuteronomy's distrust of kingship is evident. Deuteronomy sets out legislation to limit kings' authority: as we saw in chapter 2, kings cannot play any role in religious ceremonies, cannot amass or lead an army, and cannot issue legal rulings. The literary and legal parts of this book also refrain from describing God as a king. Only in one poem at Deuteronomy's end do we find the words "He became king in Jeshurun" (Deut. 33:5), which presumably relate to God; Jeshurun is a poetic name for Israel.

An examination of the four other books of the Torah compiled in Babylon and added to the book of Deuteronomy reveals a similar picture. For the most part, these books never call God a king or depict God as a king.

There are only two exceptions in the first four books, both of them also in poems:

> The Song of the Sea ends: "The Lord will reign for ever
> and ever." (Exod. 15:18)
> The Song of Balaam includes the line, "The Lord their
> God is with them, and the shout of a king is among
> them" (Num. 23:21), which also appears to refer to God.

In other words, apart from three exceptional cases, the Torah avoids the idea that God is a king. And all three exceptions occur in poems, which can be said to constitute an element external to the Torah. Many scholars agree that the poems in the Torah are older than the prose and the legislation. The poems were created orally, most likely before the eighth century BCE—that is, before the beginning of wide literacy in ancient Israel.

Moreover, as in Deuteronomy, the other books of the Torah rarely mention the idea of a kingship of flesh and blood. Although the Patriarchs received a general promise that kings would come out of them—God tells Abraham, "I will make you exceedingly fertile, and make nations of you, and kings shall come forth from you" (Gen. 17:6; see also Gen. 35:11)—nowhere in the first four books of the Torah is there a specific reference to a king who will lead the people in the future. Here, again, there is one exception, and again in a poem. The Song of Balaam apparently hints at King Saul: "His king shall be higher than Agag, and his kingdom shall be exalted (*tinase*)" (Num. 24:7). However, as we said, the poems, dated to an earlier, oral period in Israelite history, can be considered external parts which do not represent the ideology of the Torah.

Nor is the ritual of anointing with oil to be found in connection with kings in the Torah. It only appears in connection with a High Priest—for instance, in Leviticus 4:3, "If it is the anointed priest who has incurred guilt," and 6:15, "And so shall the priest, anointed from among his sons to succeed him, prepare [the offering]." This applies both to the first four books of the Torah and to the book of Deuteronomy, which rarely refer to a king of flesh and blood and never mention his anointing.

The closest figure in the Torah to a king and a Messiah, although he is not called that, is the most important: Moses. In Moses there are a number of dominant features of a king-Messiah figure. He is at the center of the greatest story of redemption in the Bible: the redemption of the people Israel from slavery to freedom. Moses also pulls off an impossible feat for an ordinary man: he remains on Mount Sinai in God's presence for many days without food or drink—"And he was there with the Lord forty days and forty nights; he neither ate bread nor drank water" (Exod. 34:28). His stay in the presence of God enabled him to overcome the bodily needs of a normal man.

Later, Exodus recounts the divine radiance that enveloped Moses because of his prolonged encounter with God on the mountain:

> When Moses came down from Mount Sinai, with the two tablets of the testimony in his hand as he came down from the mountain, Moses did not know that the skin of his face shone, because he had been talking with God. And when Aaron and all the people of Israel saw Moses, behold, the skin of his face shone, and they were afraid to come near him. (Exod. 34:29–30)

As we have seen, the purpose of anointing with oil is to impart splendor, a kind of divine radiance. Moses' divine radiance frightened the children of Israel to such a degree that he had to veil his face—only when he was in contact with God did he remove the veil (Exod. 34:33–34). Moses overcame bodily needs, was together with God, and had a divine radiance. Although he was not called a king or a Messiah, one can definitely say that he had Messiah-like characteristics.

However, a comparison of the figure of Moses in the Bible with the descriptions of kings in the Psalms reveals a very important difference. In the Psalms, the divine splendor of the kings is accompanied by eternal life. For instance:

> For thou dost meet him with goodly blessings;
> thou dost set a crown of fine gold upon his head.
> He asked life of thee;
> thou gavest it to him,
> length of days for ever and ever.
> His glory is great through thy help;
> splendor and majesty thou dost bestow
>   upon him. (Ps. 21:3–5)

In the Psalms, the king is raised above mortal men and gains eternity. In the Torah, Moses dies at age 120, although physically he was like a young man—"His eye was not dim, nor his natural force abated" (Deut. 34:7)—that is to say, he still had a great deal of vitality. It would seem that although he died at 120, his physical state would have allowed him to live a hundred years more.

The Bible scholar Samuel Efraim Loewenstamm offered a very reasonable explanation for his death at full health: namely, that this should be understood in light of the traditions concerning the sons of God found at the beginning of Genesis:[1]

> When men began to multiply on the face of the ground, and daughters were born to them, the sons of God saw that the daughters of men were fair; and they took to wife such of them as they chose. Then the Lord said, "My spirit shall not abide in man for ever, for he is flesh, but his days shall be a hundred and twenty years." (Gen. 6:1–3)

Who are these "sons of God"? The God of the Bible has no biological sons. God is above the cycle of birth, reproduction, and death.

We can best understand the sons of God as a species of second-degree divine figures. Elsewhere in the Bible, we encounter them as God's choir, praising and exalting him in song: "Ascribe to the Lord, O heavenly beings (*bnei elim*: sons of gods), ascribe to the Lord glory and strength" (Ps. 29:1); "When the morning stars sang together, and all the sons of God shouted for joy" (Job 38:7). At the beginning of Job we are also told that the sons of God assembled before God. They are always mentioned as a group, and never as individuals with names. They are different from angels (*malakhim*), who are associated with particular missions on which they are sent by God. The sons of God are a group that sits on high and sings God's praises.

The book of Genesis tells us that the sons of God saw that "the daughters of men were fair" and chose wives from among them. It does not say that this was a matter of rape or coercion, and does not use the verb *le'anot* (to violate), which appears in other cases of sexual violence. It is indeed quite possible that, just as the daughters of men were attractive to the sons of God, the sons of God were attractive to the daughters of men. But there is a problem in that this was a union of celestial beings with human beings. From a certain point of view, the union appears to have been necessary. These verses make it clear that the sons of God had sexual desires as well as the capacity to reproduce, yet according to the religion of the Bible there were no celestial women or goddesses. In other words, there were no daughters of God for them to consort with. The only outlet for the sexuality of the sons of God was with the daughters of men. But this created a difficult problem for God.

These verses come from the same source, the J source, as the Garden of Eden and the expulsion of Adam and Eve stories.[2] After Adam and Eve eat the fruit of the tree of good and evil, God is worried:

> Then the Lord God said, "Behold, the man has become like one of us, knowing good and evil; and now, lest he put forth his hand and take also of the tree of life, and eat, and live for ever." (Gen. 3:22)

The man already resembled God in knowing good and evil. Now the only thing that differentiated him from God was his mortality. If he deliberately put forth his hand to eat from the tree of life, he would gain eternal life and there would be no real difference between him and God. This was the reason why God expelled man from the garden and placed at its entrance the cherubim and the flaming sword that turned in all directions "to guard the way to the tree of life" (Gen. 3:24).

And here, in the union of the sons of God with the daughters of men, there was another possibility of eternal life. Perhaps the progeny of the sons of God and the daughters of men would be human beings who had eternal life like their forbears. This was precisely what God wanted to avoid, and so God decided:

> My spirit shall not abide (*yadon*) in man for ever, for he is flesh, but his days shall be a hundred and twenty years.

This is the only time the word *yadon* appears in the Bible, and it appears to mean "abide" or "dwell." God warned that the divine spirit, which is the source of life, would not remain with man for ever, as he was only flesh and blood, and his lifespan would be limited to 120 years.

Indeed, people more than 120 years old are only mentioned in the priestly sections of the Torah, and not in the texts belonging to the source J, who provides the stories of the sons of God and the expulsion from the garden in Genesis and the death of Moses at the end of Deuteronomy.

To return to Loewenstamm's suggestion, this could be the meaning of the description of the death of Moses at age 120. Moses appeared to have crossed the boundary between the human and the divine: he met God on the mountain, he did not eat or drink for many weeks, his face shone, and in his remarkable old age his eye was not dim nor his natural force abated. But, on the other hand, he too was flesh and blood, and therefore, despite all this, and despite the fact that from a physical point of view he could have gone on living, the text makes it clear that he was not divine but only human. The decision that "my spirit will not abide in man for ever" applied to him as well, and so he died when he reached the age of 120. The Bible sought to make a clear distinction between the human and the divine as shown in the matter of human death.

Another area in which this biblical tendency is demonstrated is in the priestly laws of purity and uncleanliness. In the book of Leviticus, we read about the uncleanliness of a woman giving birth:

If a woman conceives, and bears a male child, then she shall be unclean seven days; as at the time of her menstruation, she shall be unclean. . . . Then she shall continue for thirty-three days in the blood of her purifying; she shall not touch any hallowed thing, nor come into the sanctuary, until the days of her purifying are completed. (Lev. 12:2–4)

Thus for about forty days after the birth of a male child, a woman cannot touch a sacred object or come into the sanctuary. In the case of the birth of a female child, the period of uncleanliness is doubled (12:5). Then the woman undergoes a ritual of purification in which she offers up a lamb as a burnt offering and a pigeon or turtledove as a sin offering:

And when the days of her purification are completed, whether for a son or for a daughter, she shall bring to the priest at the door of the tent of meeting a lamb a year old for a burnt offering, and a young pigeon or a turtledove for a sin offering, and he shall offer it before the Lord, and make atonement for her; then she shall be clean from the flow of her blood.

This is the law for her who bears a child, either male or female. (12:6–7)

One may ask: Why does a woman giving birth have to provide a sin offering? What sin has she committed in bringing a child into the world?

The sages already asked this question and gave an imaginative answer. When the woman is in travail, suffering the pains of childbirth, she swears that she will never again have sexual relations with her husband. Because this vow, made when she was in labor, had to be invalidated (sexual relationships are mandatory in Jewish married life), she was asked to bring a sin offering.

But this is obviously not the plain meaning of these verses. I believe a better explanation can be found by turning to different verses in the book of Leviticus dealing with uncleanliness in sexual relations:

> If a man lies with a woman and has an emission of semen, both of them shall bathe themselves in water and be unclean until the evening. (Lev. 15:18)

According to the Bible, when a man and a woman have sexual relations—and, one must point out, here the text is speaking of permitted relations—it produces uncleanliness. The man and woman have to bathe themselves in water and wait until the evening until they are considered to be clean again. And yet the same priestly sources as those to which these verses belong also tell us in the book of Genesis that God blessed Adam and Eve and ordered them to "increase and multiply"—which shows that sexuality and reproduction are not considered bad in and of themselves.

What, then, is unclean about the man and woman after having permitted sexual relations? It seems that the true reason why both childbirth and sexual relations produce uncleanliness is once again connected with the creation of a clear distinction between God and human beings.

As Yehezkel Kaufmann pointed out, the main principle of biblical religion was the elevation of God above nature.[3] God is separate from nature and above it, and therefore not subject to the laws of nature, including the biological cycles of birth, conception, procreation, and death common to all forms of life. Because God is holy and is the source of holiness, anything other than God is tainted. In other words, the different manifestations of biological existence—birth, conception, procreation, and death—are all connected with uncleanliness because they lie outside the sanctity of God. It is not a matter of ascribing sin to sexuality as such, and here I disagree with Yehezkel Kaufmann: the increase and multiplication of human life is commendable and blessed. But, at the same time, because human sexuality is external to God, it is associated with uncleanliness, to sharpen the distinction between the sanctity of God and biological existence. The laws of purification in the Bible create a dichotomy between man who is born, gives birth, and dies, and God, who lies outside all this.

Apart from these examples, there is something else that marks the separateness of God from the biological cycle. The Torah cannot conceive that mortal man can be a "son of God," although God does have a metaphorical son: the people of Israel, called "my firstborn son" (Exod. 4:22) or "the sons of the Lord your God" (Deut. 14:1).

This also applies to Moses. We have the story of his extraordinary childhood, which, as scholars have pointed out, is paralleled in other stories from the ancient East, such as those of the kings Sargon and Cyrus. But the wonders associated with Moses are not connected to his birth, which is described as a natural event occurring to parents of flesh and blood who are even identified by name: Amram and Jochebed. Moses is not a "son of God" but the son of Amram, as the Bible states unequivocally.

Here, too, there is a great difference between the descriptions of Moses in the Torah and those of a king and a Messiah in the Psalms. In at least two places in Psalms we find descriptions of a king as a son of God. In Psalm 2, the Psalmist rails against the people and nations that appear to have been subject to the king of Judah and have now gathered together to plot a rebellion against God and God's anointed:

Why do the nations conspire,
and the peoples plot in vain?
The kings of the earth set themselves,
and the rulers take counsel together,
against the Lord and his anointed,
saying, "Let us burst their bonds asunder, and
cast their cords from us." (Ps. 2:1–3)

The Psalmist continues:

> He who sits in the heavens laughs;
> the Lord has them in derision.
> Then he will speak to them in his wrath,
> and terrify them in his fury,
> saying, "I have set my king on Zion, my holy hill."
> I will tell of the decree of the Lord:
> He said to me,
> "You are my son,
> today I have begotten you." (Ps. 2:4–7)

The king relates that God told him, "You are my son," and "today I have begotten you." Are we speaking here of a biological son of God or of a kind of adoption of the king-Messiah as a son of God?

Among Bible scholars, opinion is divided on this question. Jimmy Roberts put forward some interesting arguments against the idea of adoption.[4] In order to interpret the verse as referring to an adoption, the words "today I have begotten you" have to be understood as the Psalmist's metaphorical expression to confirm or validate the process of adoption, which begins at that moment: "Today I have begotten you." According to Roberts, the idea that the Psalmist uses a metaphor for adoption assumes that adoption was common in that society, and when people heard the words of the Psalmist, they understood what he meant.

But in that matter, there was a great difference between Mesopotamian and Israelite society. While in Mesopotamia there were very detailed and complex laws of adoption, the biblical laws do not mention the matter at all. We do have two stories of adoption—the pharaoh's daughter, who adopted Moses, and Mordechai, who adopted Esther as his daughter after her parents' death—but these were exceptional cases in special circumstances. There is no biblical story suggesting a widespread practice of adoption: a family without children adopting a child.

In view of all this, Roberts asserts that it is hard to believe that the Psalmist meant the adoption of the king; rather, the Psalmist meant to say that God literally begot him. The words we have quoted, "I have set my king on Zion, my holy hill," seem to support this reading. According to the Bible scholar Jeff Tigay the words "I have set" (*ani nasachti*) are connected with metalworking, as in the description of the golden calf (*egel masecha*) that Aaron made from the golden rings of the people of Israel (Exod. 32).[5] Both *nasachti* and *masecha* have the same Hebrew root, *nasach*. That is to say, God fashioned or made the king. Tigay points to Mesopotamian texts portraying a god fashioning kings in support of this reading.

The motif of a king begotten by God also appears in the original form of Psalm 110, a psalm both hard and important to understand in this light. The Masoretic text (i.e., the common version of the Hebrew Bible) begins as follows:

A Psalm of David.
The Lord says to my lord:
"Sit at my right hand till I make your
    enemies your footstool."
The Lord sends forth from Zion your mighty scepter.
Rule in the midst of your foes!
Your people will offer themselves freely on the day
    you lead your host upon the holy mountains.
From the womb of the dawn like dew
    your youth will come to you.
The Lord has sworn and will not change his
    mind, "You are a priest forever after the
    order of Melchizedek." (Ps. 110:1–4)

These are very profound and complex verses, but much of their content can be understood. God invites the king to sit at God's right hand, which means that the king is elevated to a semidivine status. God further promises to defeat the king's enemies.

At the same time, verse 3, "From the womb of the dawn like dew your youth will come to you," seems incomprehensible. What might these words mean?

The solution is to be found in the Septuagint translation (3rd–2nd century BCE), which renders this same verse very differently. There, God says to the king, "At dawn from the womb I have begotten you." According to this version, the king was begotten by God.

Who, then, was the feminine partner with whom God begot the king-Messiah?

Some scholars have suggested that originally the verse read, "from the womb of the dawn I have begotten you." According to this reading, the dawn served as a kind of partner-in-marriage for God. It had a human role, just as it played the role of parent in Isaiah's exclamation, "How you are fallen from heaven, O Day Star, son of the dawn!" (describing the fate of the evil king who had boasted, "I will ascend to heaven above the stars of God") (Isa. 14:12–13).

If that was the case, the king-Messiah was born from the union of God and the dawn. Then it would appear that the verse is implying that he was a kind of a heavenly creature, like a star. God begot the king from the womb of the dawn like dew. God created the king as dew comes into being in the dawn.

If that was really the original form of the verse, two questions have to be asked: First, what is the meaning of the image of "a birth like dew"? And second, why did the verse change so dramatically from its original meaning reflected in the Septuagint to the common Hebrew version, to the point that today we cannot understand it?

In order to answer the first question, we need the assistance of some ancient Egyptian texts, sometimes accompanied by illustrations, describing the birth of kings. These were generally rulers who had to find some justification for sitting on their thrones because they did not belong to the royal family or because they were female. One of them was Queen Hatshepsut, who ruled Egypt in the fifteenth century BCE. After the death of her husband the pharaoh, Hatshepsut was appointed deputy queen in order to preserve the monarchy until the pharaoh's son, the heir-apparent, grew up and took over. But Hatshepsut became fond of her role and wanted to occupy the throne of the pharaohs like all the kings of Egypt. In order to justify the unusual phenomenon of a woman ruler of Egypt, texts and illustrations were produced describing Hatshepsut's divine origins. One of the texts says that the leading god, Amun, inseminated Hatshepsut's mother with his dew, and that was how the queen was born.[6] Of course, the meaning was the god's semen, but it was described as dew.

I suggest that the author of Psalm 110 may have known this Egyptian tradition, used it, and elaborated on it. There were strong cultural relationships between Egypt and the kingdom of Judah. (For example, several chapters in the book of Proverbs are based on an Egyptian book of proverbs, the proverbs of Amen-em-ope). However, due to the theological gap between Egypt and Judah, there was no place for complete and full borrowing. Here in the psalm, in place of an actual union of the god and the queen mother, a human being, the author depicted the God of Israel as fertilizing a divine being, the womb of the morning.

Even if the author of this psalm did not intend to describe the biological birth of a king as a son of God, this is a very strange image. It could have disturbed the final editors of the Hebrew Bible who lived in the early Rabbinic period (1st–2nd century CE). Consequently, some changes were made in the text. As a result, future readers would no longer be able to discern the original meaning of the text.

One must add to this the declaration with which these verses begin: "A Psalm of David. The Lord says to my lord: 'Sit at my right hand, till I make your enemies your footstool'" (Ps. 110:1).

Compare this to Zechariah's vision in which the High Priest is invited to join the heavenly host of angels: "And I will give you the right of access among those who are standing here" (Zech. 3:7). God's invitation in the psalm is far more dramatic and audacious. It was not an invitation to stand alongside others before God, but to sit next to God. The angels stood before God and served God, but they did not have the right to sit next to God. The invitation to sit on the right hand of God gives the king, the son of God, a higher status than that of the standing angels, one that resembles that of God.[7]

Thus, the Torah as a whole, except for three poems, reflects an outlook that avoids ascribing kingship to God, is distrustful of monarchy in general, and makes a clear distinction between the human and the divine. This distinction is particularly seen in two spheres. First, while God lives forever, man is mortal. Even Moses, and even those born from the union of the sons of God and the daughters of men, had to die after 120 years, "for they too were flesh." Second, God cannot reproduce biologically, and therefore there cannot be a man who is a "son of God." At most, the concept of a "son of God" serves as a metaphor for the relationship between God and God's chosen people.

Despite this general tendency of the Torah, in the Psalms and in the words of some of the prophets there is a different tendency, in which the figure of the king is depicted as a kind of hybrid: both human and divine. In these sources, there is a glorification of the king to the point where he attains a superhuman status, both as a living king, as in the Psalms, or as a future king, as in the books of the prophets. The king is glorified in two ways to which the Torah is opposed: through a description of the king as the son of God or through giving him eternal life.

In some cases, these messianic texts external to the Torah were corrected or edited by scribes who were acting under the inspiration of the Torah, as I understand to be the case in the verses describing the king born from the union of God and the morning. The restoration of the original meaning of the verses reveals a discordance at the heart of biblical literature. It concerns the two basic views found in all the points of difference we have encountered and will continue to encounter with regard to messianism in the Bible.

One view, which the great Israeli Bible scholar Yehezkel Kaufmann described as the very basis of the biblical faith, was a belief in the inviolable distinction between divinity and humanity.[8] God transcends every aspect of biological life. The other, found in the Psalms and in the prophetic literature dealing with the Messiah, was a tendency to raise the king-Messiah above the human world, and in many respects to make him almost equal to God. As we will see, the great discrepancy between these two tendencies would continue in the following generations, culminating in the trial of Jesus before the High Priest.

7

Introducing Resurrection of the
Dead into Jewish Thought

When Zerubbabel disappeared from the historical scene in about
515 BCE, the messianic expectation of a renewal of the kingdom
of the house of David fell into a deep slumber for more than four
hundred years. This period coincided with the Hellenistic King
Antiochus's edicts of religious persecution—a very difficult time
for the people of Israel.

The only biblical book to describe the events of the period is the
book of Daniel. Written, at least in part, around the year 167 BCE,
when the edicts were promulgated, Daniel also contained a new,
innovative vision concerning the end of days: the resurrection of the
dead. In essence, this book, written after the official end of the age
of prophecy and included in the Hebrew Bible at the last minute,
served to introduce the idea of resurrection to the Hebrew Bible.[1]

To understand the genesis of Daniel, let us look at the events
in the Land of Israel from the time of Ezra (with which we ended
the last chapter).

Side by side with Ezra, Nehemiah was active in Jerusalem, serving as a governor (a Persian administrator) until 432 BCE. One
hundred years after Nehemiah, the Persian dominion over Judea
ended. In 333 BCE the army of Alexander of Macedon conquered
the Land of Israel, and some ten years later Alexander died, leaving
behind a huge empire extending from India to Greece.

Following his death, the empire was divided up among senior
officials. The Land of Judea was apportioned to the Ptolemaic
dynasty, which ruled the whole region from Alexandria (in Egypt),
but in about the year 200 BCE it fell under the rule of the Seleucid
dynasty, which ruled from Antioch (in Syria).

When the Land of Judah came under the rule of the Seleucid dynasty, the king at that time was Antiochus III, who was sympathetic to the Jews and gave them an important bill of rights. He also increased the standing of the priesthood and the authority of the High Priest, whom he regarded as the political representative of the Jewish community in the country.

In 175 BCE, his son, Antiochus IV, ascended the throne. He was called Antiochus Epiphanes (the "revealed"), because he claimed he had divine qualities and was a kind of revealed deity. This was the Antiochus who promulgated the harsh edicts against the Jews that we know about from the story of Hanukkah.

He also had far-reaching political ambitions. In two different military campaigns described in the last chapters of the book of Daniel, apparently written close to the time of the edicts, Antiochus attempted to conquer the Egyptian empire, and it seems that were it not for the intervention of the Roman fleet, which forced him to leave Egypt, he would have succeeded.[2] Shamefacedly, Antiochus had to renounce the conquest of Egypt and return to his capital, Antioch, in Syria. He promulgated his infamous edicts against the Jews when he passed through the Land of Israel on his way back to Antioch.

Because of the disguise of the book of Daniel, purported to be written by a prophet sitting in Babylon and (in its second half) having visions of what would happen at the end of days, these events were related in a coded fashion. Antiochus is called "the king of the north" and the king of Egypt is "the king of the south." After a description of Antiochus's first Egyptian campaign, the prophet depicts the king's second attempt to conquer Egypt:

At the time appointed he shall return and come into the south. . . . Ships of Kittim shall come against him, and he shall be afraid and withdraw, and shall turn back and be enraged and take action against the holy covenant. (Dan. 11:29–30)

The king of the north, Antiochus, will return to the south—that is to say, he will again turn toward Egypt—and then the "ships of Kittim" will come against him.

The meaning of "ships shall come from Kittim" is not obvious since the identity of the Kittim in the Bible is not clear; the name usually referred to nations in the area of Greece. The writer of the book of Daniel identified the Kittim with the new and rising power in the Mediterranean area, the Romans. Hence, he interpreted the old prophecy, "ships shall come from Kittim" (Num. 24:24) as referring to the confrontation of the Roman fleet with the "king of the north," Antiochus, forcing him to leave Egypt. Then "he [Antiochus] shall be afraid and withdraw, and turn back and be enraged, and take action against the holy covenant" (Dan. 11:30).

Antiochus was defeated and hurt and went back to his place. On the way back, he became angry at the holy covenant: that is to say, he directed his anger at the people of Israel:

> Forces from him shall appear and profane the temple and fortress, and shall take away the continual burnt offering. And they shall set up the abomination that makes desolate. (Dan. 11:30)

The king's representatives desecrated the Temple, suspended the daily burnt offering, and erected a Hellenistic statue (or perhaps a Canaanite one: scholars are undecided about that)—the "abomination that makes desolate"—within the Temple.

The writer of Daniel also described how Antiochus behaved with the various Jewish factions of the period:

> He shall seduce with flattery those who violate the covenant . . . and those among the people who are wise shall make many understand, though they shall fall by the sword and flame, by captivity and plunder, for some days. (Dan. 11:32–33)

Indeed, Antiochus did flatter the violators of the covenant, the Hellenizing faction in Jerusalem that supported him, while the wise among the people, the teachers of Torah to the many, fell victim to sword, fire, and captivity as a punishment for observing the commandments.

In fact, the edicts of Antiochus were something unique in the history of humanity. This was the first time in history that a ruler forbade a religion to be practiced and persecuted its adherents. Scholars are undecided about what drove him to do this. On the one hand there was his desire to be regarded as a god, and on the other the religious obstinacy of the Jews. In the background was the military defeat he had experienced in Egypt. The book of Daniel does not specify the particulars of the edicts, but from the books of the Maccabees, written in the Land of Israel and in Alexandria after the Hasmonean revolt of 167–160 BCE, we learn of prohibitions against circumcision and Torah study, and the imposition of the worship of Greek gods (see 1 Macc. 1:54–64).

Daniel also never mentions the Maccabean revolt, although scholars have detected all kinds of hints of it in the text. The book may have been written at the time of the edicts, before the revolt erupted, or it may have been written after the revolt but the author disregarded it, believing that deliverance would come from God and not from human action.

Daniel depicts the events of the time in broad historical perspective. To the prophet, the ruling kingdom of Greece has been the last—and the most wicked—of a succession of four evil empires then dominant in the world. Now, however, the events happening before his eyes will change the world order. Greece will be overthrown and severely punished. Replacing its rule will be an ideal figure, *bar enash*, the "son of man."

His night visions, as he calls them, allegorically predict this future. Four beasts emerge from the sea—the first a winged lion, the second a bear, the third a leopard. Each beast symbolizes a kingdom, and each kingdom seizes power from its predecessor. Finally, the fourth and most frightening beast emerges:

> terrible and dreadful and exceedingly strong; and it had great iron teeth; it devoured and broke in pieces, and stamped the residue with its feet. It was different from all the beasts that were before it; and it had ten horns. (Dan. 7:7)

Daniel reports that the smallest of the horns spoke boastful words. This is a reference to Antiochus Epiphanes, who boasted to be a god more powerful than the Jewish God.

Then the sea vision suddenly changes to one of the heavens above it:

> As I looked, thrones were placed and one that was ancient of days took his seat. (7:9)

The Ancient of Days was a name for the biblical God, described here more precisely than anywhere else in the Bible:

> His raiment was white as snow, and the hair of his head like pure wool. . . .
> His throne was fiery flames, its wheels were burning fire. A stream of fire issued and came forth before him; a thousand thousands served him, and ten thousand times ten thousand stood before him. (7:9–10)

Daniel is describing the heavenly retinue surrounding God, who sits on a throne erected for the Divine. God sits in judgment, passing sentences, with the books of judgment open before him:

> The court sat in judgment, and the books were opened. (7:10)

The rule of the first three beasts is usurped, though their lives are to be prolonged for a time. The fourth beast, the kingdom of Greece, is completely destroyed:

> The beast was slain and its body destroyed and given over to be burned with fire. (7:11)

Then Daniel reports a new apparition:

> Behold, with the clouds of heaven there came one like a son of man, and he came to the Ancient of Days and was presented before him. And to him was given dominion and glory and kingdom, that all peoples, nations and languages should serve him; his dominion is an everlasting dominion, which will not pass away, and his kingdom one that shall not be destroyed. (7:13–14)

A wondrous being called *bar enash*, the son of man, comes with the clouds of heaven and goes right up to God. The Ancient of Days (God) gives the son of man dominion, glory, and rule over all nations. His is an everlasting dominion. It will never cease, and his kingdom will never be destroyed.

At this point Daniel awakens. Frightened by his night visions, he asks an angel to help him interpret them. Only now, after the angel responds, does he realizes that the four beasts are four kingdoms, the horn will declare war on and defeat the holy ones (the children of Israel), but just "until the Ancient of Days came, and judgment was given for the saints of the Most High, and the time came when the saints received the kingdom" (Dan. 7:22). That is, God, the Ancient of Days, will arrive and pronounce divine judgment on the children of Israel, who will then receive the kingdom forevermore.

The book of Daniel restates this prophecy:

And the kingdom and the dominion and the greatness of the kingdoms under the whole heaven shall be given to the people of the saints of the Most High; their kingdom shall be an everlasting kingdom, and all dominions shall serve and obey them. (7:27)

To understand the significance of *bar enash*, we have to look closely at the angel's interpretation. Since the four beasts were four kingdoms, and the last one Greece, which persecuted the people of Israel, it follows that *bar enash*, to whom "was given dominion and glory and kingdom, that all peoples, nations and languages should serve him . . . an everlasting dominion," was the people of Israel. That is to say, *bar enash* appears not to be a particular man, but a collective representative of the people of Israel.

Not all scholars accept this interpretation. Some scholars think that *bar enash* should be identified with the archangel Michael, whom the book of Daniel depicts as the heavenly representative of the people of Israel (see Dan. 10:11). I do not think that this interpretation is in agreement with these verses, but, whatever the case, according to many scholars, *bar enash* refers to a collective representative of the people of Israel. Just as each of the beasts represented a nation, so the "son of man" represented an entire people, Israel.

This understanding also figures into the beginning of the heavenly vision in which Daniel saw thrones, in the plural ("thrones were placed"), with God sitting on one of them. If there were two thrones, who was the other throne meant for? Who sat on it? From the context, many scholars and commentators have thought that *bar enash* sat on the other throne. That is to say, the representative of the collective people of Israel sat next to God in heaven.

In the last chapter, we saw that in the Psalms, the king, a messianic figure, was invited to sit next to God in heaven:

Sit at my right hand, till I make your enemies your footstool. (Ps. 110:1)

Daniel appears to have taken hold of this messianic image and applied it to the whole people of Israel.

One should remember that the book of Daniel does not mention the Messiah as a son of David, and does not speak of former rulers of the house of David or a future revival of the monarchy. In fact, the book's only two mentions of a Messiah (again, meaning "anointed one") refer to a High Priest anointed with oil: "To restore and build Jerusalem to the coming of an anointed one"; "An anointed one shall be cut off, and shall have nothing" (Dan. 9:25–26). The first mention appears to refer to Joshua ben Jehozadak, the High Priest at the time of the return to Zion, and the second to Onias III, a High Priest killed in Antioch in the second century BCE.

Thus, from a certain point of view, the book of Daniel can be seen as an antimessianic work. The writer of the book does not expect a Davidic Messiah, and appears to subject messiahship to a kind of democratization. In place of the Messiah, Daniel seats beside God the whole people of Israel, represented by the "son of man." Likewise, he transfers the promise of eternal rule—given in the Psalms and the Prophets to a king of the house of David—to the "son of man," the people as a whole.

In this respect, there is a similarity between the book of Daniel and the prophecies of the second Isaiah, who also abandoned the hope of reviving the house of David, and who transferred the promises made to David, the "mercies of David," to the whole people: "and I will make an everlasting covenant with you, my steadfast mercies of David" (Isa. 55:3).

At the same time, parallel with the democratization of messiahship in Daniel is an important phenomenon that contradicts the Torah's principle of making a clear distinction between the human and the divine. I refer to the special vision of the resurrection of the dead.

It must be stressed that the idea of the resurrection of the dead does not appear in a clear, literal form anywhere in the Hebrew

Bible except in the book of Daniel. Chapter 37 of the book of Ezekiel includes the image of dry bones that revived—"and the breath came into them, and they lived" (Ezek. 37:10)—but as Ezekiel 37:11 explicitly says, this is a symbolic vision of the resurrection of the despairing people: "These bones are the whole house of Israel. They say, 'Our bones are dried up, and our hope is lost; we are cut off completely.'" Again, a clear declaration in the Hebrew Bible that the dead will be resurrected in the future can only be found in Daniel, chapter 12. In fact, elsewhere, in several places, the Hebrew Bible says that the path to Sheol (a place of darkness where the dead go) is one-directional: whoever goes down there can never return.[3]

By contrast, in his vision of the future end of days, Daniel says:

> At that time shall arise Michael, the great prince who has charge of your people. And there shall be a time of trouble, such as never has been since there was a nation till that time; but at that time your people shall be delivered, every one whose name shall be found written in the book. And many of those who sleep in the dust of the earth shall awake, some to everlasting life, and some to shame and everlasting contempt. And those who are wise shall shine like the brightness of the firmament; and those who turn many to righteousness, like the stars for ever and ever. (Dan. 12:1–3)

After a great tribulation, unparalleled in the past, the dead will be resurrected and will be judged after their death.

While the idea of a judgment after death is not known to us anywhere else in the Hebrew Bible—in other words, Daniel introduces this motif single-handedly—it does appear in the Egyptian and Persian religions. As Daniel presents it, among "those who sleep in the dust" and will arise, some will gain eternal life, and some, eternal shame and contempt. But the teachers of Torah whom Daniel mentioned previously and are here called wise will have a divine splendor for ever and ever.

Likewise, in this vision there is a kind of democratization of the messianic idea, for, as noted, the anointing of the Messiah with oil gives him a divine splendor, and he indeed sometimes resembles a star, as in the verse "A star shall come forth out of Jacob" (Num. 24:17, which we will meet again later). Here the divine splendor and star-like radiance are given to a whole group: the wise and the teachers of the Torah who were tortured and killed, and will be resurrected in the future and have a heavenly status like stars or angels.

In order to understand this first appearance of the idea of the resurrection of the dead in Daniel, we must realize the intensity of the religious crisis in that generation, connected with the doctrine of reward. The biblical understanding of reward had trained believers to expect rewards for observing the commandments and punishments for transgressing them, as the verses say again and again. Thus, for example, Leviticus 26 describes what will happen "if you walk in my statutes and observe my commandments and do them" (Lev. 26:3): the people will have rain, an abundance of agricultural produce, peace, and so on. But "if you will not hearken to me, and will not do all these commandments" (26:14), the people will be afflicted with sicknesses, drought, military defeats, and more. This condition recurs innumerable times in the Bible.

However, this conception of reward and punishment is questioned in various places. Thus, for example, in the book of Job the issue is discussed as Job receives no answer to the question of why bad things happen to good people.

Yet in the generation of the author of Daniel, there was a new problem, one more serious than anything before: that of righteous people who were enduring pain and suffering not *despite* the fact that they observed the commandments but *because* they did so. The man who persisted in teaching Torah, who circumcised his son and refused to worship idols, was the one who was made to suffer—tortured, killed, or burned—precisely because he observed the commandments. And the reverse was also true: the sinners who adopted Greek customs and transgressed the commandments received political and economic benefits from the Greek authorities.

In essence, the civil laws against the observance of the religion nullified the biblical doctrine of reward and punishment, provoking a profound religious crisis. That was the background to the dramatic innovation of the writer of the book of Daniel, one unequaled in the Pentateuch or anywhere else in the Bible: the idea that there is a life after death, including judgment and reward for the things one does in one's life. The principle of reward comes into play after death: the wicked are judged and are sentenced to eternal disgrace, while the righteous—the teachers and observers of the Torah—receive abundance and eternal life.

To sum up, it could be said that in one respect the book of Daniel is an antimessianic work, inasmuch as it makes no mention whatsoever of the hope of a revival of the kingdom of the house of David. Daniel does take from the Messiah tradition messianic features such as sitting next to God and shining with divine splendor, but bestows these on Israel as a whole, apparently represented by the "son of man." On the other hand, with its novel doctrine of reward, the book of Daniel undermines the Torah's sharp distinction between God and humanity. The idea that after death some humans will have eternal life largely effaces the distinction between humans and God.

The innovations advanced by the book of Daniel were not accepted by all factions of the Jewish people, as we will soon see. At least a portion of the people totally rejected belief in the resurrection of the dead and the doctrine of reward. The group of deniers would come to play a central role in the trial of Jesus.

8

The Sadducees' Denial of the
Doctrine of Reward

The pertinent, divergent texts in the Bible we have discussed so far would have profound, indelible influence upon the sects of the Second Temple period and beyond. One such sect was the Sadducees, a priestly group living in Jerusalem about two hundred years before its destruction.

The Sadducees were an elite group of priests. They were born into aristocratic families, the wealthier elements of the population. The High Priest came from this group. Usually they maintained good connections and relations with the Roman rulers. They were very strict on issues of purity and impurity, while they rejected belief in resurrection and angels.

Challenging our deeper understanding of this group is that they left no writings whatsoever. The Sadducees disappeared from Jewish history with the Temple's destruction in 70 CE—apparently many were killed in the great rebellion that preceded the devastation. While in the writings of the sages there are references to Sadducee works such as the "Sadducee Book of Edicts," even if there was such a book, and even if some copies had the good fortune to survive the great fire in the Temple, nothing has reached our hands. Unlike the writings of the Qumran sect, which have come down to us owing to dry conditions in the desert regions in which the sect was active, the works of these city dwellers were not preserved for us in the damp climate of Jerusalem.

In the absence of primary sources provided by the Sadducees themselves, we have to learn about them from the writings of others, some of whom—like the Rabbis or sages of the talmudic era and the early Christians—were their opponents. The Pharisees and the sages who came after them accepted the Oral Law, which the Sadducees rejected. The sects also disagreed on many legal and theological issues, foremost for our purposes, resurrection of the dead, which the Pharisees and the sages accepted and the Sadducees spurned. This issue was also at the heart of the debate between the Sadducees and the early Christians.

One of the main sources we possess—and the closest Jewish source contemporaneous to the events—is the writing of Josef ben Mattityahu, better known as Josephus Flavius, a Jewish historian who was active at the time of the Jewish war against Rome (66–70 CE) and who later went to Rome and wrote his great works (*The Jewish Wars, Jewish Antiquities*). Additionally, we have multiple references in the literature of the sages, which itself came into being several hundred years after the Sadducees, and thus may not accurately depict the sect. Other references to the Sadducees appear in the writings of the Qumran sect, in the New Testament, and in other Christian works, especially those known as pseudo-Clementine, which describe, among other things, the disputes between the Sadducees and the Christians. When we read works in these traditions, we must always remember that all the historical descriptions, and certainly those written with a purpose, such as to promote their own views and to correspondingly denigrate the antithetical views of their opponents, are liable to be slanted and biased.

We shall begin our investigation of the Sadducees with the works of the sages, which preserve various traditions concerning their world. While the passage of several hundred years between the events and sages' reportage of them, as well as the aforementioned biases, give us reason to adopt a skeptical, critical attitude to the texts, at the same time, when a description or a particular detail appears in a number of different sources, we can give it more credence and assume that it has a historical basis.

Let's begin with a teaching from Pirkei Avot (Ethics of the Fathers) that does not mention the Sadducees specifically, but brings us rapidly into their presence:

> Antigonus of Sokho received this from Simon the Just. He said, Be not like servants who serve their master for the sake of reward; rather, be like servants who do not serve their master for the sake of reward. (Pirkei Avot 3:1)

This was a saying of Antigonus of Sokho (a settlement in Judea). Simon the Just, mentioned here as his master, appears to have been the High Priest Simon, son of Honias the First, who lived at the end of the third century BCE. In the book of ben Sira, a whole chapter is devoted to a story from the life of this High Priest.

The fact that a Jew born in the small Judean settlement of Sokho at the beginning of the second century BCE was given the Greek name "Antigonus" shows the depth of the penetration of Hellenistic culture in Judea. A hundred and thirty years after Alexander of Macedon had conquered the Land of Israel, it seems that Hellenistic culture was having considerable influence on the Jews, or at least on some of them.

We do not know if, apart from his name, Antigonus was exposed to Greek philosophy and the ancient Greek outlook, but scholars have discussed his very interesting saying a great deal, among other things with regard to its affinity with Greek wisdom. Antigonus told his disciples not to serve God "in order to receive a reward"—that is, not to work for wages—but to do so like servants who serve their master without any expectation of reward. In some versions of the saying, the command is expressed in even stronger terms—not "not in order to receive a reward," but "in order not to receive a reward": that is to say, with the ideal of not receiving a reward. Whatever the case, in Antigonus's opinion, the observance of the commandments should not be connected with the expectation of a reward from God.

A midrash called *Avot DeRabi Natan*, which amplified Pirkei Avot and was ascribed to Rabbi Natan, a sage from Babylon who lived in Galilee in about 200 BCE, had this comment about the saying we have read:

Antigonus of Sokho had two disciples who used to study his words.

They taught them to their disciples, and their disciples to their disciples.

These proceeded to examine the words closely and demanded: "Why did our ancestors see fit to say this thing? Is it possible that a laborer should work all day and not take his wages in the evening?"[1]

These punctilious disciples raised objections. Why did Antigonus of Sokho ask us to be like servants who do not expect a reward? Is it logical that a laborer who works all day does not receive his wages in the evening?

They came to the following conclusion:

If our forefathers knew that there is another world and there is a resurrection of the dead, they would not have said this.[2]

In other words, Antigonus said it because he did not believe in the world to come and the resurrection of the dead—a belief that, as we saw in the last chapter, had been represented for the first time in the book of Daniel.

The midrash continues:

So they arose and withdrew from the Torah and formed two groups, the Sadducees and the Boethians.

The group known as Boethians was apparently close to the world of the Sadducees. According to the above account, the schism of the Sadducee sect from mainline Judaism took place at the time of the disciples of Antigonus of Sokho's disciples ("They taught them to their disciples, and their disciples to their disciples").

Can we date the schism described in these Rabbinic sources? According to the Mishnah, Yossi ben Yoezer of Tzereidah, a disciple of Antigonus of Sokho, was killed during the edicts of Antiochus,[3] which would date him to about 170 BCE. The period of the disciples of Antigonus's disciples was the generation after Antiochus III's edicts against the practice of Judaism—that is to say, the beginning of the Hasmonean period: about 150 BCE.

The dating of the Sadducean schism is also confirmed by a theological disputation recorded in the midrashic tradition. As we saw in the last chapter, the innovation of the book of Daniel with regard to the resurrection of the dead grew out of the need to resolve a great crisis of faith concerning the doctrine of reward. In the period of the edicts, during which Antigonus's disciple Yossi ben Yoezer of Tzereidah and many of the "punctilious" disciples were killed, some very difficult questions arose. The people of the time saw with their own eyes how those who sacrificed their lives to observe the Torah suffered terrible tortures and were killed, while the Hellenistic sinners who accepted the Greek religion were in comfort and had the support of the authorities. This was the background to the assertion in the book of Daniel: yes, the historical reality did not correspond to the classical doctrine of reward, but the many blessings that the Bible promises the observers of the commandments would still come to pass, not in the present life but in the life after death.

How did the contemporaries of the book of Daniel react to this? Did they accept the offered solution? And, if not, how did they deal with their crisis of faith?

I would like to suggest that this was precisely the background against which the tradition of the sages on the Sadducean schism and the controversy concerning the resurrection of the dead has to be seen.

This idea is also supported by Josephus Flavius's discussion of the outlook of the Sadducees. Josephus describes their outlook in two places: in book 2, sections 164–65 of *The Jewish Wars*, and in book 18, sections 15–17 of *Jewish Antiquities*. According to him, the Sadducees believed that humans are given freedom to choose between good and evil; God does not see human actions and does not guide humanity. The Sadducees did not believe in the immortality of the soul and in reward and punishment after death. Thus, according to Josephus, they did not accept divine providence or the doctrine of reward:

> The Sadducees . . . do away with Fate altogether, and remove God beyond . . . the very sight of evil. . . . As for the persistence of the soul after death, penalties in the underworld, and reward, they will have none of them.[4]

Here there is complete agreement between the literature of the Sages and Josephus's historical descriptions of Saducean theology.

In light of this, I claim that the Sadducees refused to accept the solution proposed by the book of Daniel. They rejected the doctrine of afterlife reward grounded in the ideas of the resurrection of the dead and the immortality of the soul. Moreover, there developed among them the idea that commandments should not be performed "in order to receive a reward."

Even as the Sadducees rejected ideas of divine Providence as well as reward and punishment, they were very strict in observing the law. The halakhic tendency of the Sadducees is supported by archaeological findings. In Nahman Avigad's 1970s excavations of the Jewish quarter in the Old City of Jerusalem, among the splendid houses of the Second Temple period to be revealed were homes belonging to priests who were part of Sadducee circles. On the floor of one such house in the Jewish quarter was a stone inscribed with "Bar Katros," the son of Katros. Katros was the name of a well-known priestly family. More generally, in the ruins, evidence showed that although these were homes of wealthy families, the dishware in daily use was not made of precious metals, as have typically been found in the kitchens of other Jewish families of means from this period, but of stone. The vessels, trays, and so on were all of stone.

The reason was that, according to the halakhah, stone vessels (unlike ones of ceramic and metal) are not infected by impurities such as impure animals, dead creatures, etc. It appears that these Sadducee-priestly circles were very scrupulous in matters of purity and uncleanliness.

Given their strict adherence to law in these matters, it is reasonable to think that their departure from accepted teaching was limited specifically to their disagreement concerning the theological questions of reward and the resurrection of the dead.

This dispute can be considered from another angle. The Sadducee position resonates with an early priestly tradition described in my book *The Sanctuary of Silence*.[5] Following Yehezkel Kaufmann, I argued there that the "priestly Torah," the theological outlook of a group of priests, focused on a ritual system that was not intended to obtain material wealth or success. The rituals of the priestly Torah did not include ceremonies for rain, sacrifices when going into battle, or rituals for healing the sick. Rather, the purpose of the ritual system was to gain closeness to God.[6] Thus already in the priestly tradition there existed the kernel of the idea that divine commandments should not be performed in order to obtain a reward.

With that background, we can see how a combination of two elements likely led to the formation of the Sadducee worldview. First, the historical event of the edicts against the practice of Judaism—practice that consequently became a source of hardship—caused a certain group of priests to adopt and develop the incipient idea already contained in the ancient priestly tradition, of a religious ritual "not in order to receive a reward." Why did the Sadducees reject the resurrection of the dead, as proposed by Daniel, which provided a delayed reward to substitute for the earthly one? Because of the second key element: the Sadducees' fidelity to the Torah's position maintaining a clear distinction between the human and the divine. If humans were endowed with eternal life after death, as the book of Daniel proposed, the huge difference between the divine and the human would be eclipsed.

This is in keeping with another piece of evidence we have concerning the Sadducees. The New Testament says that the Sadducees did not believe in angels (Acts 23:8). In this matter, too, they were in the line of the priestly Torah, which does not mention angels. By not accepting the existence of intermediary beings who belonged both above and below, the Sadducees were preserving the barrier between God and human beings.

It would seem that all we have learned here about the Sadducees explains another fact concerning their outlook. Of all the Jewish groups active at the end of the Second Temple period, the Sadducees are the only one in which there is no hint of messianic expectation. Messianism is present in the writings of the Qumran sect, in the ideas of the Pharisees, and of course in the Christian view. This important point bears repeating: Based on the evidence we have, the Sadducee sect is the only movement of the period in which there is no suggestion of messianic faith.

All this is of course interconnected. One who does not believe in Providence or divine reward cannot have any hopes of future redemption through God or God's representative. In such a view of history, there is no stage in which the righteous will be rewarded with redemption for their faithfulness to God. Moreover, the Sadducees' seeming refusal to close the gap between God and humans also distanced them from the messianic idea, at the center of which was a semidivine figure sometimes identified in the Psalms and the writings of the prophets as God's son. Such a figure did not fit the Sadducee's careful exclusion of God from the human sphere and biological cycles of birth, sexuality, and death.

In a certain way, then, by adopting these two principles, the Sadducees continued the classical view of the Torah, which stressed the difference between God and human beings and avoided messianic expectations for the future. As we will soon see in greater detail, however, the Sadducees' ideas would clash with those of their contemporaneous and geographical neighbors: the people of the Qumran sect, the Pharisees, and the first Christians. The discordance between the nonmessianic Sadducee approach and the messianic approaches that sprang up around it would come to its peak during the trial of Jesus.

9

Qumran Accounts of an Exalted and Suffering Messiah

Although the Sadducees did not accept the idea of a Messiah and rejected beliefs in divine providence and the resurrection of the dead, shortly after their appearance the messianic hope for a king of the house of David suddenly reemerged.

As we have seen, the hope for a Messiah of the Davidic line lapsed and fell into a state of slumber in about the year 515 BCE, with the disappearance of Zerubbabel ben Shealtiel, the heir to the house of David in whom hopes had been placed at the time of the return to Zion. For four hundred years, all such aspirations were centered instead in the leadership of the priesthood and the anointed High Priest. A Messiah of the house of David did not appear in the texts dating from that period, including the book of Daniel, which contained a turbulent vision of the end of days and the resurrection of the dead.

It wasn't until about the year 100 BCE that the idea of a Messiah of the house of David reappeared: in the writings of the Qumran sect on the shores of the Dead Sea. The scrolls of this sect—the first of the Dead Sea Scrolls to be found—were discovered in 1947. A Bedouin shepherd was trying to bring a goat that had strayed into one of the Judean desert caves near the shores of the Dead Sea back to the herd. When he threw a stone into that cave, he heard the sound of it hitting a clay pot. After descending into the cave—with great difficulty; the cave is in a steep slope of a canyon—he found several clay jars containing seven scrolls.

The Bedouins then sold these scrolls to "Kando," as the antiquities dealer preferred to be identified at the time, although his real name was Iskandar. An Assyrian Christian who had fled from

Turkish persecution in his hometown of Tur Abdin in Turkey in the first decades of the twentieth century, Iskander was now both a shoemaker and an antiquities dealer in Bethlehem.

A few years ago, Iskander's son told me the backstory of the sale of the scrolls. Members of the Bedouin Ta'mireh tribe came to his father the shoemaker with the scrolls they'd found and asked him to use the leather of which they were made to make them sandals. To our good fortune, Iskander knew how to read Aramaic, the liturgical language of the Assyrian church, to which he belonged. The Aramaic and the Hebrew script are identical, hence Iskander could easily read the Hebrew scrolls, and he recognized their antiquity. He sold four of them to the metropolitan Mar Samuel, the head of the Assyrian church in Jerusalem.

Iskander sold the other three scrolls to Eliezer Lipa Sukenik, an archaeologist at the Hebrew University (and father of the famous archeologist Yigal Yadin), who saw that they were ancient writings thousands of years old. Several years later, in 1954, nearly all of the most important complete scrolls reached the Israeli scholars. Later, more scrolls were added to them and many fragments of scrolls as well.

Some of the Qumran scrolls are biblical texts that constitute important corroborative evidence of the authenticity of the traditional version of the Bible. Until the discovery of these scrolls, the oldest known manuscript of the Hebrew Bible was the Aleppo Codex written in the ninth century CE. Here, suddenly, were examples of biblical texts more than a thousand years older than the Codex, dated to approximately between 200 BCE to 50 CE.

Apart from the biblical texts, some of the scrolls contain *pesharim*—interpretations of biblical texts by members of the Qumran sect. In addition, the scrolls detail the rules and regulations of the sect—which had a communal life—and many visions of events at the end of days, along with other of the sect's general beliefs.

In matters of divine Providence and reward, the people of the Qumran sect took a position opposite to that of the Sadducees.

Whereas the Sadducees denied Providence and reward, members of this sect denied free will and believed in predestination. All that happened on earth was predetermined by God's will, they believed, and no one could oppose it. Moreover, God had predetermined that part of humanity would belong to the "sons of light," who were righteous, and another part would belong to the "sons of darkness," who were under the "rule of Belial." The sect also had a special calendar.[1] Since Qumran members believed that anything relating to the moon was connected to the rule of night and the forces of darkness, they therefore followed a solar calendar. By contrast, other Jewish groups used a lunar-solar calendar, similar to the current Jewish calendar.

Today, most scholars believe that the people of Qumran were identical with the "Essenes," mentioned by Josephus Flavius, the Hellenistic Jewish philosopher Philo of Alexandria, and the Roman historian Pliny the Elder. These authors described the Essenes as active from about the first century BCE through the first century CE—the same time period as the established dating of the Dead Sea Scrolls—and as centered near the Dead Sea. Like the members of Qumran, the Essenes believed in predestination and in the eternity of the soul. Both also rejected private ownership and lived communally. Both took daily ritualistic baths and maintained very high levels of physical purity. Hence, it is reasonable to identify one with the other.

In order to understand the historical context in which the Qumran/Essene sect operated, let's look for a moment at the central aspect of their self-image: their sense of being a group that broke away. Members of the sect described themselves as having broken away from the mainstream: "We broke away from the majority of the people."[2] When did that happen, and for what reason?

There were, of course, practical reasons for the separation, like its distinct calendar. Qumran/Essene members observed the biblical holy days, but according to a different calendar. You could not be part of the people if, when you were celebrating Passover and eating matzot (unleavened bread), the rest of the people were behaving as if it were an ordinary day and eating regular bread. And of course you could not share in running the Temple in such circumstances.

And, apart from this, there might have been another reason for the schism—an external one, connected with Jewish politics in the Land of Israel. In the past, many scholars suggested that the breakaway happened at the beginning of the Hasmonean period, after Hasmonean rule had been established. According to this theory, when, in about 159 BCE, Jonathan, the brother and successor of Judas Maccabeus, took on the title of High Priest, the people of Qumran opposed it. They, who belonged to the major, original line of priests, as they saw it, would have objected to an unimportant priestly family from the town of Modi'in taking the leadership of the priesthood. This theory is supported by the fact that Josephus Flavius's *Jewish Antiquities* refers to the Essenes in its account of the period of Jonathan the Hasmonean.

But this explanation is problematic for two reasons. First of all, as the scholar Joseph Sievers has pointed out, the passage in *Jewish Antiquities* in which Josephus mentions the Essenes has no relation to its context.[3] It appears to have been placed there in order to fill a gap in the work, and therefore has no value as evidence from Josephus. Second, and more important, even though there are many polemics in the scrolls against the Hasmonean rulers, nowhere are the rulers blamed for taking the nomination and honor of High Priesthood for themselves. Since elsewhere the Qumran writings detail disputes with other sects, the lack of such findings here is suspicious.

And in fact, in recent years scholars have pointed to certain signs that the Qumran writings were not composed around the year 150 BCE but fifty years later, around the year 100 BCE. The excavations at Qumran under the American archaeologist Jody Magness have shown that the settlement was founded around 100 BCE and not earlier. An examination of the Dead Sea Scrolls by Carbon 14, a method of radiometric dating, has dated the sectarian texts to no earlier than around 100 BCE.[4]

Third, a study of the historical events in the writings of the sect, seen in relation to our historical knowledge of the period, and especially the writings of Josephus Flavius, places the earliest texts of the sect in the period of Alexander Jannaeus (103–76 BCE). For example, one scroll relates the Pharisees' inducement of the Seleucid king Demetrious III to fight against Jannaeus, and Jannaeus's revenge, the crucifixion of eight hundred Pharisees.

If this dating is correct, we have to return to the question we asked earlier: do we know of any political events that happened in the area around 100 BCE that could have led to the breakaway of the members of the sect?

In this matter, I would like to build on the ideas of the Israeli historian David Flusser and claim that the breakaway was connected to the fact that around the year 100 BCE the Hasmoneans began to call themselves kings.[5] There is conflicting evidence concerning the first leader to do this: whether it was Aristobulus I, who ruled for one year from 104 BCE to his untimely death, or his brother Alexander Jannaeus, who married his brother's widow, Queen Salome Alexandra, and replaced him on the throne. Whatever the case, it was in about the beginning of the first century BCE that the Hasmoneans first assumed the title of kings.

What is more, it appears that this very event formed the background to the reemergence of a competing conception: the hope for a Messiah from the house of David. In their writings, Qumran members specifically declared that a monarchy had to be directly connected to the tribe of Judah (to which David's house belonged). They based this on Jacob's blessing of Judah in the book of Genesis: "The scepter shall not depart from Judah, nor the ruler's staff from between his feet" (Gen. 49:10). One Qumran text serving as a kind of commentary on the book of Genesis reads:

The scepter shall not depart from the tribe of Judah, whenever Israel rules, there shall not fail to be a descendant of David upon the throne . . . until the Messiah of Righteousness comes, the Branch of David, for to him and his seed is granted the Covenant of kingship over his people for everlasting generations.[6]

Thus, a king who was not of the house of David—and the Hasmoneans were not—could not be appointed. The covenant of eternal kingship had been made with the Davidic dynasty.

The Davidic messianism suddenly awoke from its peaceful slumber because someone wished to harm it. In my view the Hasmonean ruler who took the title of king upon himself thereby provoked the secession of the Qumran sect.

In quite a number of writings from Qumran, one may find, next to the royal figure from the House of David who is a political leader, a priestly figure whose chief role is to teach the Law. Such depictions have been found in the Damascus Covenant Scroll, a Dead Sea Scroll so named because it speaks about the community of covenant living in Damascus (scholars do not know if Damascus was a symbolic name to the Qumran sect or whether the Qumran community really lived in Damascus for a while). In this scroll's interpretation of the passage in Balaam's prophecy, "A star shall come forth out of Jacob, and a scepter shall rise out of Israel" (Num. 24:17), we read: "The scepter is the community's leader and the star is the interpreter of the Law." The scepter symbolizes the authority of the community's political ruler, who has to be from the house of David, and the star is the priestly ruler, who expounds and teaches the Law.

Another Qumran text interprets the passage in which God says to David, "I will be his father, and he shall be my son" (2 Sam. 7:14) to mean that "he is the Branch of David who will arise with the interpreter of the Law"—that is, that in the future a Branch of David will arise, and, next to him, a priestly leader who, here too, is called an "interpreter of the Law."[7]

As Shemaryahu Talmon and other scholars have pointed out, these Qumran texts revert to the dual model of messianism of the period of the return to Zion: the two Messiahs (anointed figures), the political and the priestly; the "two sons of Yitzhar" of the book of Zechariah.[8]

At the same time, in other Qumran texts the matter is less clear. For instance, the problematic words "the Messiah of Aaron and Israel" appear elsewhere in the Damascus Covenant Scroll. These words can be read as a description of two different Messiahs, one from Aaron and one from Israel—that is to say, a priestly Messiah and a national/political one—but they can also be interpreted as describing a single figure who is a Messiah of both Aaron and Israel.

Whatever the case, it is clear that monarchical messianism, associated with the line of the house of David, was resurrected in the writings of Qumran. In some cases, this messianism has a military, triumphal character. Like David, the warrior-Messiah, the Messiah is depicted many times as a victor who defeats his enemies in battle. Thus, for example, the "Rule of the Blessings," a kind of addendum to the regulations of the sect (the "Community Rule") that contains blessings on both the political leader and the priest, says this with regard to the royal political leader who will arise at the end of days:

> May He make your horns of iron and your hooves of bronze. . . . For God has established you as the scepter. The rulers . . . [and all the kings of the] nations shall serve you. He shall strengthen you with His holy Name and you shall be as a lion.[9]

The leader is blessed to be victorious over his enemies and, moreover, to overcome them like a lion. In fact, this is a kind of return to the biblical model we find in the Psalms: a strong warrior-Messiah who overcomes Israel's enemies.

But the Qumran literature also includes another image of a leader who is to a large extent the opposite of the warrior-Messiah:

a messianic figure characterized by suffering and atonement for the sins of others. Before we consider the appearance of this figure in Qumran literature, let us recall the biblical roots of the idea that the coming of the Messiah will atone for the sins of the whole people. In the book of Zechariah, when the prophet speaks of the arrival of "my servant the Branch," he says, "I will remove the guilt of this land in a single day" (Zech. 3:9) But he never explains how such an atonement, which would absolve the land in a single day, would come about, or the connection between the atonement and the arrival of the messianic figure. We shall therefore look at three examples of the connection between messianism, suffering, and atonement in the writings of Qumran.

The first appears in the Great Isaiah Scroll. Found in the jars in the cave at Qumran, it contains the whole of the book of Isaiah, but in a somewhat different form from the one we had. One of the differences concerns the figure of the suffering servant in the prophecy of the Second Isaiah. Let us look again at the beginning of the prophecy about the servant as it appears in the book of Isaiah:

Behold, my servant shall prosper, he shall be exalted and lifted up, and shall be very high. As many were astonished at him—his appearance was so marred, beyond human semblance, and his form beyond the sons of men—so shall he startle many nations; kings shall shut their mouths because of him; for that which has not been told them they shall see, and that which they have not heard they shall understand.

Who has believed what we have heard? And to whom has the arm of the Lord been revealed? For he grew up before him like a young plant, and like a root out of dry ground; he has no form or comeliness that we should look at him, and no beauty that we should desire him. He was despised and rejected by men; a man of sorrows and acquainted with grief; and as one from whom men hide their faces he was despised, and we esteemed him not. Surely he has borne our griefs and carried our sorrows, yet we esteemed him stricken, smitten by God and afflicted. But he was wounded for our transgressions, he was bruised for our iniquities; upon him was the chastisement that made us whole, and with his stripes we are healed. All we like sheep have gone astray; we have turned every one to his own way; and the Lord has laid on him the iniquity of us all. (Isa. 52:13–15; 53:1–6)

The Second Isaiah depicted the servant as a despised, sick, and suffering man whose sufferings were not incurred by his sins. This man took the sins of others upon himself. He "was bruised for our iniquities," and with his "stripes" and his sufferings, all of us were healed.

As we saw in chapter three, the vision of the suffering servant had already raised questions in ancient times. Who was this servant? Who were the sinners he was atoning for? Was he an individual or did he represent a collective, and if he was an individual, who could it be?

From textual analysis, as we saw in chapter 3, it seems clear that although the figure of the servant in the Second Isaiah sometimes represents the prophet, in the specific case of the vision of the suffering servant, it is not a personal portrait but a collective image of the people of Israel or the righteous among them. According to this view, the sinners for whose sins the servant atones were the nations of the world who had committed the sin of idolatry. Indeed, many of the Second Isaiah's prophecies were intended to open the eyes of the nations and rescue them from the darkness of idolatry. The prophet describes how in the future the nations of the world will see the suffering servant and understand that he was suffering for them in order to atone for their sin of idolatry. Again:

But he was wounded for our transgressions, he was bruised for our iniquities; upon him was the chastisement that made us whole, and with his stripes we are healed. (Isa. 53:5)

This interpretation, which many major scholars support, is quite convincing. We know that the Jewish community in Babylon was perturbed by the question of the meaning of their own suffering and punishment. In the book of Lamentations, the complaint is expressed in a very strong form—"Our fathers sinned, and are no more; and we bear their iniquities" (Lam. 5:7)—and in the book of Ezekiel we also find the famous figurative expression of this idea: "The fathers have eaten sour grapes, and the children's teeth are set on edge" (Ezek. 18:2). Wasn't Jerusalem destroyed because of the sins of the kings who practiced idolatry, and especially those of King Manasseh, who was mentioned specifically in this connection (2 Kings 21:1–13)?

But Manasseh remained long on his throne and died in peace, whereas it was the people of the next generation who were exiled and suffered. Where, then, was divine justice? The figure of the suffering servant described by the Second Isaiah offered a possible solution to this problem. The suffering was not due to the sins of the fathers or those of the sons. It was due to the sins of the nations of the world, which the people of Israel bore and for which they themselves atoned.

In other words, we can rule out an Israelite messianism here. The suffering servant in the Second Isaiah was a collective figure representing the people of Israel or the righteous among them, and therefore could not be an individual Messiah. As we saw earlier, the Second Isaiah used the term "Messiah" for Cyrus, a foreign king, and bestowed the "mercies of David" on the entire people (Isa. 45:1; 55:3). For the Second Isaiah, the Persian king Cyrus was the Messiah, the "mercies of David" were given to the whole people, and the figure of the suffering servant was a collective image of the people or the righteous people among them, assuaging the sufferings of Israel.

But when we look at the Isaiah scroll preserved at Qumran, we observe a slight difference that changes the whole picture. In the traditional Jewish text (the Masoretic text), one of the verses describing the servant reads:

As many were astonished at him—his appearance was so marred beyond human semblance (*ken, mshhat me ish marehu*), and his form beyond that of the sons of men. (Isa. 52:14)

In the Qumran version, however, an additional letter is added to *mshhat* ("marred") so the word becomes *mshhahti* ("I have anointed"):

ken, mshhati meish marehu (also I have anointed his [the servant's] image)

According to the Qumranic version, the Prophet is saying that God anointed the servant.

As the eminent philologist Yechezkel Kutscher claimed, and as did other scholars who worked on this scroll, this was not a textual error.[10] The writer from the Qumran sect wanted to give the servant a messianic character. In his opinion, the suffering servant did not represent Israel as a collective, but was an individual, suffering Messiah who took the sins of others upon himself and atoned for them.

Does this discovery have a broader context? Can one point to other writings of the Qumran sect in which there is a suffering figure who atones for others, comparable to Isaiah's suffering servant? The answer to these questions is yes, and I wish to indicate two such texts.

In the heart of the first text, written in Aramaic and, unfortunately, only available to us in fragmentary form, a priestly persona appears. The text describes the extraordinary wisdom and abilities of this hero of the composition:

His word is like a word of heaven, and his teaching is according to the will of God. His eternal sun will shine, and his fire will spring forth to all the ends of the earth, and will shine over darkness until the darkness will pass away from the earth.[11]

This description of the sun shining until the darkness passes away recalls another composition of the Second Temple period, not from Qumran: the Testament of Levi, which forms part of a larger work, the Testaments of the Patriarchs, a pseudepigraphic book that lists the testaments of Jacob to his sons. Fragments of this work were found among the works preserved in the sect's library, it contains a description of a future priest who resembles the one in our text:

> Then shall the Lord raise up a new priest to whom all the sayings of the Lord will be revealed, and he will do true justice on earth at the end of days. Then his star will rise in the sky like the star of a king, and he will illumine with the light of knowledge as the sun lights up the day and he will increase in the earth. He will shine like the sun upon the earth and banish all darkness under the heavens, and there will be peace throughout the earth. (Testament of Levi, 2–4)

The Qumran text Rule of the Blessings includes a similar blessing on a priest at the end of days:

> And may he make you holy among his people, and an eternal light to illumine the world with knowledge and to enlighten the face of the congregation with your teaching.[12]

But in the Qumranic Aramaic text with which we are concerned, there are other motifs not found in the Testament of Levi or the Rule of the Blessings: the suffering and afflictions of the priestly hero, for one, and the fact that he atones for the sins of his generation, for another. The priest's suffering is described in a figurative way: "your blood and your pain."[13] The text also says that "he is not indebted"—that is, the suffering figure has not sinned. Although he is sinless, he endures afflictions nonetheless. This description undoubtedly corresponds to that of the suffering servant who takes the sins of others upon himself and suffers on their behalf.

Further on in the text, the priest suffers from nonphysical afflictions as well: "Lies and falsehoods will be told about him, and all kinds of accusations will be made about him."[14] The priest endures shame and contempt, just like the suffering servant in Isaiah: "He was despised and rejected by men" (Isa. 53:3). And like the suffering servant, the suffering priest in the Qumran document "atoned for all the members of his generation."[15]

The great, erudite Joseph Baumgarten, who founded the study of the Halakhah of Qumran, claimed that the atonement brought by the priest was not connected with sacrifices but rather by his suffering. Like Isaiah's suffering servant, the priest atoned by suffering for all the members of his generation.[16]

Here we should remember that already in the Pentateuch there was a hint that a High Priest atoned for the sins of others by his death. The law concerning the cities of refuge said that an unintentional killer had to escape to a city of refuge and to live there "until the death of the high priest" (Num. 35:25). My teacher Moshe Greenberg suggested that the suffering and death of the High Priest atoned for the sins of the whole country and all members of the generation, including the unintentional killer, who could now go home.[17]

Another figure with whom we are concerned appears in a special and unusual text from Qumran about which a great deal has been written, and which I too have dealt with in my book *The Messiah before Jesus*.[18] The text consists of two psalms. In the first, the writer praises and exalts himself. The second is a communal psalm in which the community gives thanks for elevation of the figure in the first psalm.

The text of the two psalms is found among the writings of Qumran in two versions. The first is in the Scroll of Thanksgiving, a scroll of psalms that appears to have been written, at least in part, by the "teacher of righteousness," the leader of the sect. The second may have formed part of the scroll of The War of the Sons of Light against the Sons of Darkness, although there is some dispute among scholars about this. Whatever the case, what is of interest to us is the extraordinary juxtaposition in the first psalm: the writer exalts himself and praises his virtues on the one hand and speaks of his degradation on the other.

The most surprising line in the psalm is when the writer says about himself, "Who is like me among the gods?"[19] He is taking the verse in the Song of the Sea, "Who is like thee, O Lord, among the gods [*elim*]?" (Exod. 15:11), and applying it to himself. Note, though, that in Qumran terminology, the word *elim* (gods) means angels. The writer is therefore saying that there is no one like him among the angels. He is above them.

This is the most extraordinary statement in all of Qumran literature, which generally displays a desire to join the angels, to sing with them and to praise God. This is the only place in Qumran literature where it is claimed that someone is above the angels. Moreover, the writer also boasts that he sat on a heavenly throne: "For I sit on my [throne] in heaven."[20] He describes the throne on which he sat in heaven as "a throne of power in the angelic council." That is to say, he sat there as the angels stood surrounding him. This description is even more exaggerated, because the writer is comparing himself to God. Angels were not allowed to sit, and their standing around God, who was seated, symbolized their subjection to the Divine. Here, the writer himself was sitting on the throne, surrounded by angels.

But, as well as being raised to a heavenly condition, this leader was the victim of abuse. He said, "Who has been despised like me?"[21] and "Who compares to me in enduring evil?"[22] At the same time as being quasi-divine and declaring "Who is like me among the gods-angels?," this writer suffered, was afflicted, and was an object of scorn and derision to those around him, just like Isaiah's suffering servant.

In addition to this psalm, there is, as we said, another psalm in this text, one in which the community gives thanks for the elevation of the suffering, godlike leader. As a result of his appearance, "wickedness perishes . . . grief disappears and groaning flees; peace appears, terror ceases . . . iniquity ends, plague affliction ceases, so that there is no more sickness; injustice is removed, and guilt is no more."[23] While the speaker in the first hymn compares himself to Isaiah's suffering servant, in the second hymn the community declares that "iniquity ends." The connection between the two contrasting statements is probably this: just as in Isaiah's prophecy the suffering servant atones for the sins of others, here, too, the suffering and grief of the leader brings about a situation in which "iniquity ends." It seems, then, that this exceptional text from Qumran was in keeping with the small emendation we have seen in the Isaiah Scroll, in which the word *mshhat* ("marred") in the description of the suffering servant was changed to *mshhahti* ("I have anointed"), thus giving the suffering servant a messianic character. Finally, it must be pointed out that the depiction of a suffering leader who atones with his sufferings for those of his generation was exceptional in the world of the Dead Sea Scrolls. Most of the texts describe the Messiah in the form found in the Bible: a strong, victorious personality. But the minority view of an exalted Messiah who sat on a heavenly throne yet suffered and thus atoned for those around him was an important one destined to play a central and meaningful role in the birth of Christianity.

The Pharisees' Expectations of an Imminent Messiah

In the Second Temple period, yet another Jewish group was active: the Pharisees. Unlike the Sadducees, who were mainly located in Jerusalem (near the Temple), and members of the Qumran sect, who were mainly in the Dead Sea area, the Pharisees were to be found everywhere in the Land of Israel, and they had great influence on Jewish society.

The name of the group—Pharisees, in Hebrew *prushim* (abstainers)—was connected with the need to distinguish its members from the rest of the people, whom Pharisaic leaders viewed as the *Am ha-Aretz* (the common people) in matters of purity, cleanliness, and other commandments about which the Pharisees themselves were particularly strict. They differed from the Sadducees and the Qumran sect in their belief in the sanctity of an oral law passed from generation to generation. While few Jews strongly identified with the group in the sense of abiding by its many special restrictions with regard to purity and cleanliness, the writings of Josephus Flavius, the Dead Sea Scrolls, and the New Testament tell us that most of the people followed the Pharisees nonetheless. The multitudes came to rely on the Pharisees, in large part because Pharisaic rituals and prayers expressed the anticipation that God would save and bless the people in their times of need and distress. Thus for instance the people supported the Pharisees' newly established rituals for Sukkot—water libation and the circling of the altar with willow branches—even though these rites were not mentioned in the Torah and therefore both the Sadducees and the Essenes rejected them. The people were predominantly pragmatic: these observances were meant to produce rain needed for their crops.[1]

In effect, the Pharisees, Sadducees, and Essenes were all opponents vying for the Jewish people's loyalty. The Pharisees gained the greatest number of supporters because they spoke to the essential physical as well as spiritual needs of the people. Later, after the destruction of the Temple, when the Sadducees and members of the Qumran or Essene sect had disappeared from history, the Pharisees remained the dominant movement of the Jewish people, and it was among them that the world of the sages with its religious creativity came into being. Generally speaking, the Pharisees of the late Second Temple period became the sages after the Temple's destruction in 70 CE.

Prior to the destruction, the Land of Israel was part of the world conquered by Alexander the Great of Greece. When the Hellenistic King Antiochus IV issued religious decrees prohibiting the people from practicing Judaism and desecrated their Temple, the Jews rose in revolt. The Hasmonean rebellion started around 166 BCE. Led at first by Mattathias of the priestly Hasmonean family and then by his son Judah the Maccabee, the Jews entered Jerusalem and purified the Temple (events now commemorated yearly on the festival of Hanukkah).

At first the Hasmoneans called themselves High Priests. However, as we have seen, around the year 100 BCE they started taking the title of king. Presumably this act led members of the Qumran sect, which believed that kingship should be reserved only for the tribe of Judah, to reject of the legitimacy of the Hasmonean monarchy. Like the Qumran adherents, the Pharisees opposed the Hasmonean monarchy, albeit not consistently. At first, early in the rule of John Hyrcanus I (134–104 BCE), the Pharisee-Hasmonean relationship was more harmonious. Both the sages and Josephus Flavius tell us that the Pharisees initially admired John Hyrcanus. The Pharisees called him John the High Priest and spoke favorably about him. But later on their relationship ruptured following an interesting episode.

One of the Pharisees said that John Hyrcanus should stop serving as High Priest. He based his assertion on a rumor—that Antiochus Epiphanes' soldiers had imprisoned John's mother during the Hasmonean revolt—and because there was a suspicion that she had been raped by them, her offspring could not serve in the Temple. Josephus Flavius, describing this affair, said that as a result John Hyrcanus changed sides and became a Sadducee, and that both he and his successor, Alexander Jannaeus, had difficult relations with the Pharisees and persecuted them.[2] Only after Alexander's death, when his widow, Salome Alexandra, ascended the throne, did relations improve. (The Talmud tells us she was a sister of the great Pharisee Shimeon, son of Shatah, but we cannot establish the historical validity of this story.)

Beyond the somewhat similar attitudes of the Pharisee and Qumran communities to the Hasmonean monarchy, there was another, more consistent, point of similarity: both groups' expectation of the appearance of a Messiah of the house of David.

Before we delve into this development, I need to make a methodological observation. The problem in investigating the Pharisees' positions is that hardly any Pharisee texts have come down to us. Like the sages who continued their path, the Pharisees favored oral teaching. They believed it was forbidden to write down their teachings, chiefly because of the necessity of preserving a clear distinction between the written Torah—that is, the Five Books of Moses—and the interpretations different scholars and Rabbis were giving to the Torah texts. Thus the descriptions we have of the Pharisees come to us mainly from external sources, such as the works of Josephus Flavius (who spent some time with them) and the very polemical writings of the Qumran sect. In the Dead Sea Scrolls the Qumran authors denigrate the leader of the Pharisees as "the preacher of falsehood" and "the man of jest." Polemical descriptions of the Pharisees also appear in the New Testament, generally in connection with their disputes with Jesus, which we will explore in the following chapters. Additionally, the Pharisees are represented in the literature of the sages, often in sayings attributed to earlier sages such as Hillel and Shammai. Yet the reliability of these Pharisaic traditions is also uncertain because of the distance in time between the historical events (from around 40 BCE) and their written documentation (around 500 CE).

At the same time, fortunately, we do possess two exceptional works written in Pharisee circles before the destruction of the Temple. The first is Megillat Taanit (the Scroll of Fasting), which lists the memorial days in the Jewish calendar. The original version of the text appears to have been written at the end of the Second Temple period.

The other work, which is central to our concern, is called the Psalms of Solomon.

A collection of psalms ascribed to King Solomon, the Psalms of Solomon has come down to us in the Greek language. For many years scholars thought that it was originally written in Hebrew and then translated into Greek. More recently, the Bible scholar Jan Joosten has asserted that its author was a Jew who came to Jerusalem from the Greek-speaking community in Alexandria in Egypt, and so the work was in fact originally composed in Greek.[3] This idea, for which Joosten has provided compelling evidence, changes the picture with regard to an important matter to be discussed later in this chapter.

Written around the middle of the first century BCE, the Psalms of Solomon relates to two historical events we will discuss further on, in 66 BCE and 48 BCE respectively. One may conclude from this that the work was written after 48 BCE, or perhaps the psalms were written in stages in the course of the first century BCE. No Pharisee sages are mentioned in the work, but among scholars it is seen, broadly speaking, as reflecting the world of Pharisee thought. Even if the writer did not strictly observe all of the sect's religious prescriptions and did not belong to its inner circle, he is identified with the Pharisees on account of his ideas. Unlike the Sadducees, who denied the existence of Divine Providence and the principle of reward, and unlike the members of the Qumran sect, who believed in predestination, the writer of the Psalms of Solomon believed in Providence and in reward and punishment. Hence, his spiritual world is seen to have been that of the Pharisees. As such, this work is the chief evidence we have of the Pharisees' views with regard to a Messiah.

The Psalms of Solomon lambasts the Hasmoneans for unlawfully appropriating the kingship promised to the house of David. Psalm 17 declares that God chose David and promised that his progeny would rule forever:

> You, O Lord, you chose David king over Israel,
> and you swore to him concerning his offspring forever,
> that his palace would never fail before you.
>   (Ps. of Solomon 17: 4)

Then the psalm describes the crisis surrounding the Hasmonean monarchy:

> And, because of our sins, sinners rose up against us;
> they attacked us and thrust us out, to
>   whom you did not promise;
> they took possession by force, and they did
>   not glorify your honorable name.
> They set up in glory a palace
>   corresponding to their loftiness;
> they laid waste the throne of David in arrogance
>   leading to change. (Ps. of Solomon 17:5–6)

The Hasmoneans took by force something they had not been promised. "They set up in glory a palace corresponding to their loftiness," and in so doing they destroyed the throne of David.

Thus, the writer says, God will make sure that a foreign leader rises up and gives the Hasmonean rulers the punishment they deserve:

> But you, O god, will overthrow them and will
> remove their offspring from the earth
> when there rises up against them a person
> that is foreign to our race.
> According to their sins you will repay them, O God,
> that it may befall them according to their
> works. (Ps. of Solomon 17:7–8)

The person "foreign to our race" was the military commander Pompeius Magnus, also known as Pompey the Great, an ally of Julius Caesar, who later became his bitter rival. In the period we are concerned with, Pompey was the Roman Empire's representative in the Middle East. He had come to the region to deal with pirates who were interfering with maritime trade, and remained there for a few years.

It was precisely in this period that Queen Salome Alexandra died and her two sons contended for the succession. According to the law of the firstborn, her eldest son, Hyrcanus, should have ascended the throne, but her younger son, Aristobulus, who was more combative and energetic than his brother, wanted the kingship for himself. In the ensuing conflict, both sides turned to the Roman representative in the region, Pompey, for support. For his own reasons, Pompey decided to support Hyrcanus, and in 63 BCE he came to Jerusalem to fight against Aristobulus. For three months he lay siege to the city, while Aristobolus's supporters fortified themselves in the Temple Mount area. Finally, the Roman soldiers breached the walls surrounding the Mount, entered the

Temple and the Holy of Holies, causing a great shock among the people, and took Aristobulus and his sons to Rome in chains behind Pompey's chariot in a victory procession.

The writer of the Psalms of Solomon saw this degradation of Aristobulus the Hasmonean as God's punishment of the Hasmonean kings for usurping the throne of the house of David:

> Faithful is the Lord in all his judgements
>   which he performs in the earth. . . . .
> The lawless one [Pompey] . . . laid waste our land
>   so that no one inhabited it; they destroyed
>   young and old and their children together.
> In the wrath of his beauty he expelled . . .
>   them to the west [to Rome],
> and the rulers of the land to derision, and did
>   not spare them. (Ps. of Solomon 17:10–12)

Elsewhere, in Psalm 2, the writer describes Pompey's desecration of the Temple:

> Foreign nations went up to your altar;
> in pride they trampled it with their sandals,
> because the sons of Jerusalem had defiled
>   the sanctuary of the Lord,
> had profaned the gifts of God with acts of
>   lawlessness. (Ps. of Solomon 2:2)

Later on, the writer mentions the prisoners ("The sons and daughters were in harsh captivity," 2:6) and the acts of rape ("The daughters of Jerusalem were profane," 2:13)—the latter also mentioned in the writings of Josephus Flavius.

On the other hand, the writer also describes the punishment inflicted on the Roman conqueror:

Do not delay, O God, to repay them on their heads,
to declare in dishonor the arrogance of the dragon.
And I did not wait long until God showed
  me his insolence, pierced,
on the mountains of Egypt. (Ps. of Solomon 2:25–26)

In 48 BCE, Pompey was near the coast of Egypt, in the area of the
city of Pelusium (Baluza in Arabic), and close to nearby Mount
Casius. He was induced to come down to the coast, ostensibly in
order to meet some people who wished to pay their respects to
him, but in fact this was a trap set by Julius Caesar's supporters.
When Pompey approached the coast he was murdered, and thus
Caesar became the sole ruler of the Roman world.

The struggle between the Hasmonean brothers continued, and
each one tried to engage the support of a foreign power. Aristobulus, and his heir Mattathias Antigonus, gained the assistance of the
Parthian kingdom, and the Romans continued to help Hyrcanus.
Finally, as a result of this perpetual conflict, in 40 BCE, Herod,
who was not a Hasmonean but Edomite in origin, came to power
in Jerusalem (already his father Antipater was the chief adviser of
Hyrcanus). In other words, Herod was of foreign origin and ruled
by grace of the Romans, who dictated what happened in the Land
of Israel through him. That is how the Hasmonean line came to an
end, and that was also the end of independent Jewish rule, which
had begun with the Maccabean revolt in 167 BCE.

These events gave rise to messianic hopes in the writer of the
Psalms of Solomon: now a ruler from the house of David would
appear, fight against the enemies of Israel, and restore Jewish
independence to its former glory.

The writer's portrait of this imagined ruler gives us a glimpse
of an ideal messianic figure as seen by a Pharisee writer of the
mid-first century BCE:

See, O Lord, and raise up for them their king,

the son of David,
at the time which you choose,
O God, to rule over Israel your servant.
And gird him with strength to shatter
    in pieces unrighteous rulers,
to purify Jerusalem from nations that trample her
    down in destruction. (Ps. of Solomon 17:21–22)

The future ruler would be a king of the house of David. A mighty warrior, he would crush "unrighteous rulers" and cleanse Jerusalem from the nations that trampled it underfoot,

in wisdom of righteousness,
to drive out sinners from the inheritance,
to smash the arrogance of the sinner like a potter's vessel,
to shatter all their substance with an iron rod, to destroy
    the lawless nations by the word of his mouth,
that, by his threat, nations flee from his presence,
and to reprove sinners with the thought of
    their hearts. (Ps. of Solomon 17:23–25)

This passage emphasizes two elements, each of which reflects a different biblical source. The first is the king's warlike capacity, which, the writer hopes, will "smash the arrogance of the sinner like a potter's vessel, shatter all their substance with an iron rod." This description is clearly based on Psalm 2 in the book of Psalms, in which, as we saw, God tells a king: "You are my son, / today I have begotten you" (Ps. 2:7), and that, when this king fights against his enemies, "You shall break them with a rod of iron, / and dash them in pieces like a potter's vessel" (Ps. 2:9). The words in the Psalms of Solomon, "Smash the arrogance of the sinner like a potter's vessel, / shatter all their substance with an iron rod," echo the verse in Psalm 2 but reverse the order of its two parts, a known practice in biblical borrowings.[4]

The second element in the passage is the king's capacity "to destroy the lawless nations by the word of his mouth, that, by his threat, nations flee from his presence." This verbal facility is reminiscent of another messianic text in the Bible: the prophet Isaiah's image of the Messiah from the house of David: "And he shall smite the earth with the rod of his mouth, and with the breath of his lips he shall slay the wicked" (Isa. 11:4). Thus the writer of the Psalms of Solomon combined the physical prowess of a king-redeemer with miraculous aspects of Isaiah's image.

Clearly, part of the king-Messiah's task is to fight against the other nations and expel them from Jerusalem. In contrast to the biblical messianic model of Isaiah and his followers, in which *God* is the military redeemer and the future Messiah is meant to establish righteousness and justice, the writer of the Psalms of Solomon holds that one of the king's duties is to fight against his enemies. This element is also found in some of the Qumran texts, in which, in addition to a celestial war involving angels, the head of the community, the "shoot of David," fights and kills the leader of his enemies. The Psalms of Solomon show that this view, which gives the future king-Messiah the mission of achieving victory over the Romans and redeeming the people of Israel, was also that of the Pharisees. Inasmuch as broad sections of the people followed the Pharisees, this view no doubt was widely influential.

I would like to dwell on another messianic element in this Pharisaic text, appearing in a verse whose meaning has been disputed. The verse describes the king-Messiah as follows:

And he shall be a righteous king,
taught by God, over them,
and there shall be no injustice in his days in their midst,
for all shall be holy, and their king the Lord-
  Messiah. (Ps. of Solomon 17:32)

Particularly interesting here are the final words, "And their king the Lord-Messiah," which gives the Messiah the name of God.

Some scholars, like Joseph Klausner and Menahem Stein (Stein translated the Psalms of Solomon from Greek to Hebrew) have claimed that this is a Christian distortion of the original text.[5] According to them, the work, which the Church preserved, was subject to deliberate Christian editing. In accordance with its view that Jesus was the incarnation of God, the Church introduced the term "Lord-Messiah" here. Other scholars who hold that the present Greek text is a translation from the original Hebrew believe that it originally read, "And your king is the Messiah of the Lord," but the Greek translator misunderstood the meaning, transposed the words, and inadvertently created the expression "Lord-Messiah."

In this matter, I am inclined to agree with the scholars Bird and Write that this was not a case of mistranslation or of Christian editing.[6] As mentioned earlier, the scholar Jan Joosten has demonstrated convincingly that the work was not translated but originally written in Greek, so the mistranslation hypothesis has to be rejected. This was apparently the original form of the text. But, if so, how could that be? How could the writer elevate a Messiah of flesh and blood so far as to give him the name of God?

The answer is very clear. In fact, we know that this was nothing exceptional. We saw in the prophecies of Jeremiah that he called the future king "the Lord our righteousness":

Behold, the days are coming, says the Lord, when I will raise up for David a righteous Branch, and he shall reign as king and deal wisely, and shall execute justice and righteousness in the land . . . *And this is the name by which he will be called: "The Lord our righteousness."* (Jer. 23:5–6, italics added)

As we have also seen, Jeremiah followed Isaiah's way of speaking of the future leader as "Mighty God" (Isa. 9:6). The Psalms of

Solomon were written in a period when the prophetic books were already canonized, so it is reasonable to assume that their author was well acquainted with the book of Jeremiah and followed in the prophet's footsteps.

A careful scrutiny reveals other parallels between the verse and the passage from Jeremiah. Jeremiah describes a king as "a righteous branch," and the writer of the Psalms of Solomon speaks of "a righteous king." Jeremiah prophesies that "the king will execute justice and righteousness in the land," and the Psalms of Solomon declares, "There shall be no injustice in his days in their midst." Jeremiah calls the king "the Lord our righteousness," and the author of our psalm calls him "their king the Lord-Messiah."

In other words, this Pharisee writer was assuring his audience that a Messiah—in fact, a semidivine Messiah—of the house of David would soon arrive to put things right. The Roman conquest of Jerusalem—the killing of thousands of Jews and the defilement of the Temple—induced the author of the Psalms of Solomon to expect divine intervention. God would send a Davidic Messiah who would defeat the Romans and redeem the people of Israel.

Finally, indications of a concept of a warlike Messiah can also be found in the historical environment close to the Psalms of Solomon. A few decades after it was written, on the feast of Purim in 4 BCE, Herod, the king who ruled Judea by the grace of the Romans, died. A month later, thousands of people gathered in Jerusalem and filled the Temple in celebration of the feast of Passover. A delegation representing the people approached Herod's successor Archelaus and presented him with demands for reforms in government and a reduction of taxes. When their demands did not meet with a suitable response, a great rebellion broke out in the Temple courtyard and quickly spread throughout the country. There were three focal points in this rebellion, and each of them had a different leader. Two of the leaders, Simon of Peraea, active beyond the Jordan and in the Jericho area, and a man called Athronges, active in the area of the Jerusalem Hills, declared themselves kings. (Historians are not certain what happened immediately thereafter. Internal battles may have raged for several months before the Romans arrived to quash the many-sided rebellions.)

It is plausible to think that these two military leaders held the view of the Messiah's mission as expounded in the Psalms of Solomon and adopted it for themselves. Each of them thought that he was the king who would fight against the Romans and liberate Jerusalem and the whole of the Land of Israel from its enemies. In some respects, these obscure commanders were the first messianic leaders in history to seek restoration of the Jewish people's political freedom in the Land of Israel.

Varus, the Roman governor of Syria, cruelly suppressed the revolt against Herod's successor. Arriving in the area in 4 BCE with several legions, he destroyed and burned Zippori (Sepphoris), the center of the revolt in the Galilee. From there, Varus went on to Judea, occupying Jerusalem and crucifying thousands of people around the city walls. These battles, known as "the war of Varus," took place in 4 BCE, which also appears to be the date Jesus of Nazareth was born. Jesus was probably born in Nazareth, very close to Zippori (Sepphoris), the center of the Galilee revolt, at the very time of the "war of Varus." Thus Jesus was born in a traumatic area and time.

The Pharisees' conviction regarding the imminent arrival of a Messiah of the house of David—a semidivine Messiah at that—would flare up at some of the trials of Jesus's followers.

Jesus's Messianic Conception

Jesus was born around 4 CE, about the time of Herod's death and the rebellion against Rome (both 4 BCE), and grew up in Nazareth following the trauma of civil unrest and political upheaval. His name—Yeshua in Hebrew, meaning "salvation"—was common at the time, a symbol of the Jewish people's hope of redemption.

His father, a carpenter, died when he was a boy. As the oldest son of four brothers and several sisters (Matt. 13:55–56), Jesus replaced him as the family breadwinner by doing carpentry work for the people of the village. Jesus appears to have been close to his family in those early years, but these ties were severed after John the Baptist baptized him in the River Jordan.

John the Baptist, a preacher and a spiritual leader, worked in the area close to the river. There he baptized thousands of Jews who flocked to him to confess their sins, repent, and purify themselves. John was calling for Israel's repentance. He promised the people of Israel that if they repented and were baptized, they would be saved from the wrath of the Last Judgment at the end of days. From Ezekiel 36:25 he could draw the idea of ritual cleansing as a condition for redemption; the text teaches that purification in water should be accompanied by repentance and a change of heart. Among the great many who came to be baptized and saved from the Last Judgment was the approximately thirty-year-old Jesus.

The earliest of the New Testament's four gospels, Mark, does not suggest any personal connection between John and Jesus at the time of Jesus's baptism. This impression is confirmed by a story in Matthew 11:2–6, in which John sent messengers much later to inquire into who Jesus was.

As he was baptized, Jesus heard a voice saying to him: "Thou art my beloved Son; with thee I am well pleased." He also saw the Holy Spirit descending on him in the form of a dove (Mark 1:10–11). After this experience, Jesus seems to have regarded himself as the Messiah anointed by the Holy Spirit. He returned to Nazareth with this conviction. Invited to read the haftarah (chapter from the Prophets) in his family's synagogue in Nazareth on the Sabbath, Jesus proceeded to read verses 1 and 2 from Isaiah, chapter 61:

> The Spirit of the Lord is upon me, because he has anointed me to preach good news to the poor. He has sent me to proclaim release to the captives and recovering of sight to the blind, to set at liberty those who are oppressed, to proclaim the acceptable year of the Lord. (Luke 4:17–19)

After Jesus finished the reading, he said to the people in the synagogue:

> Today this scripture has been fulfilled in your hearing. (4:21)

In other words, Jesus was convinced that *he* was the one whom the Holy Spirit had anointed in the Jordan in order

> to preach good news to the poor. . . . He has sent me to proclaim release to the captives and recovering of sight to the blind, to set at liberty those who are oppressed. (Isa. 61:1)

The people of his town strongly disapproved of this messianic declaration, to the point that they tried to kill him by throwing him off a mountain (Luke 4:23). As we will soon see, like most of the Jews in this period they were waiting for a royal Davidic Messiah, who in their eyes would not have come to them in the figure of this simple carpenter.

Escaping from his assailants, Jesus fled to the northwest of the Sea of Galilee in the area of Capernaum and Chorazin, where he was not known and there were no prejudgments against him. Soon he became occupied with healing the sick and casting out devils (Mark 1:29–5:43). Then, Mark tells us, a dozen people who were impressed by his words and abilities became his disciples, following him as he journeyed from town to town, touching and healing people struggling with illnesses and praying on their behalf. Some of his disciples helped Jesus in his healing acts (Mark 3:13–19).

Members of his family heard about his exploits. Concerned that he might have gone out of his mind, his mother and brothers made the journey to ask him in person to return to his family, but Jesus refused to see them, saying that his disciples were now his true family (Mark 3:21, 31–35; Matt. 12:46–50). Jesus also told his disciples to leave their families (Matt. 19:29). He declared that he had come to break up, not unite families (Matt. 10:34; Luke 12:51–52), and even said that anyone who did not hate his family could not be his disciple (Luke 14:26). It was said that Jesus once refused to allow a disciple to go bury his father (Luke 9:59–60), and he did not allow another disciple to say a farewell to his family before leaving them (Luke 9:61–62).

As much as his new family of disciples esteemed him, they also misunderstood him. His disciples shared the Jewish people's Pharisaic belief in a warrior-Messiah. They expected Jesus to behave accordingly and deliver the nation from Roman rule, as this later reflection attests:

We trusted that it had been he which should have redeemed Israel. (Luke 24:21)

In another example of the people's perspective, when Jesus is approaching Jerusalem before Passover, a blind beggar sitting on the roadside near Jericho cries out to him:

Jesus, Son of David, have mercy on me! (Mark 10:47)

To the people, here represented by the beggar, Jesus is the expected kingly Messiah of the house of David.

However, Jesus saw himself quite differently. The Gospels say he revealed a secret to his disciples: that he was a Messiah of another kind, a suffering Messiah:

> And he began to teach them that the Son of man must suffer many things, and be rejected by the elders and the chief priests and the scribes, and be killed, and after three days rise again. (Mark 8:31)

One of his disciples, Peter, rebuked Jesus after he said this:

> And [Jesus] spake that saying openly. And Peter took him, and began to rebuke him. (Mark 8:32)

Still, Jesus continued to view himself as a suffering Messiah. On his way to Jerusalem before Passover, he would utter his most explicit reference to himself as a suffering servant committed to relinquishing his life to atone for others:

> The Son of man came not to be served but to serve, and to give his life as a ransom for many. (Mark 10:45)

The gap between the mighty expectations of the people and the humble Jesus is also seen in the way Jesus approached Jerusalem from the Mount of Olives: riding on an ass (Mark 11:1–5 and parallels). Jesus, who knew the prophetic books very well, apparently sought to adopt the image of the humble king riding on an ass, as in the prophecy of Zechariah:

Rejoice greatly, O daughter of Zion! Shout aloud, O daughter of Jerusalem!

Lo, your king comes to you. He is just and has salvation, lowly and riding on an ass. (Zech. 9:9)

Still, the people around him continued to speak of Jesus as a typical Davidic king-Messiah:

And those who went before and those who followed cried out, "Hosanna! . . . Blessed be the kingdom of our father David that is coming! Hosanna in the highest!" (Mark 11:9–10).

Hosanna means "save us." The people surrounding Jesus expected him to save them within the context of the coming "kingdom of our father David." Even the disciples failed to understand what Jesus said about a suffering Messiah:

He said to them, "The Son of Man is going to be delivered into the hands of men. They will kill him, and after three days he will rise." But they did not understand what he meant and were afraid to ask him about it. (Mark 9:31–32)

The discrepancy between how Jesus saw himself and how the people saw him is less surprising given that Jesus himself always asked his disciples to keep the idea of Jesus as a suffering Messiah a secret:

"But what about you?" he asked. "Who do you say I am?" Peter answered. "You are the Messiah." Jesus warned them not to tell anyone about him. He then began to teach them that the Son of Man must suffer many things and be rejected by the elders, the chief priests and the teachers of the law, and that he must be killed and after three days rise again. (Mark 8:29–31)

Does this tradition, according to which Jesus only shared the secret of a suffering Messiah with his disciples, have a historical basis? Discussing this question in his book, *The Messianic Secret*, the early twentieth-century German New Testament scholar William Wrede argued that the tradition about the messianic secret was simply a fabrication devised by the early church after Jesus's crucifixion in order to have the narrative conform to the tragedy of the crucifixion.[1] According to him, the historical Jesus did not see himself as a suffering Messiah and never spoke about it; no one ever heard anything about it from him in his lifetime. In order to hide this fact, the early church claimed that Jesus had asked for the doctrine of the suffering Messiah to be kept secret.

One of the main contentions of Wrede and the scholars who followed him was that Jesus could not have spoken of a suffering Messiah, because the proud Jewish mentality of his period would not have allowed for such a figure. As we've discussed, the Jews of Jesus's time expected a heroic Messiah: a victorious warrior-king like David who would fight against the Roman enemy and deliver the people of Israel from their submission to Rome. This was the messianic hope of the Pharisees and of the masses of people who followed them. This would ostensibly have been the original messianic conception of Jesus's Galilean disciples.

However, the discovery of the Dead Sea Scrolls has dramatically expanded scholarly acquaintance with the variety of messianic positions held by different Jewish groups at the end of the Second Temple period. As we saw, three Qumran texts present the idea of an unusual messianic figure who is both exalted—elevated to a quasi-divine status—and suffering. And like Isaiah's suffering servant, he also atones for all the members of his generation.

In one of the texts, the priestly hero's sufferings are described figuratively: "your blood . . . the blows of your pain."[2] This text also pronounces that "you are not guilty"—that is, the suffering figure is sinless as he endures afflictions. This is like Isaiah's suffering servant who takes the sins of others upon himself and suffers on their behalf: "He was wounded for our transgressions; he was bruised for our iniquities" (Isa. 53:5).

Later in the Qumran text, the priest suffers from nonphysical afflictions: "Lies and falsehoods will be told about him, and all kinds of accusations will be made about him."[3] The priest endures shame and contempt, just like the suffering servant in Isaiah: "He was despised and rejected by men" (Isa. 53:3). And like the suffering servant in Isaiah, "with his bruises we are healed" (Isa. 53:5), the suffering priest in the Qumran document "atoned for all the members of his generation."[4]

Could Jesus have been exposed to this messianic conception of the members of the Qumran sect? The beginning of Jesus's view of himself as the Messiah took place with his baptism by John the Baptist in the River Jordan. In order to conduct these baptisms John was traveling the length of the Jordan, from the Dead Sea area in the south to the shores of the Sea of Galilee in the north, in the Dead Sea area. According to the Israeli historian David Flusser, he appears to have met people from Qumran. Flusser even thinks John the Baptist was a member of the Qumran sect for a time until he broke away because of ideological differences.[5] This might explain the exceptional importance of baptism in Qumran praxis and in the circle of John. Perhaps, as Flusser has suggested, John served as a channel, bringing Jesus ideas from Qumran.[6]

Jesus's baptism in the River Jordan could be a confirmation of the influence of Qumran on Jesus's perception of himself. As mentioned, Jesus announced that at the time of his baptism, the Holy Spirit descended on him and he heard a voice giving him the elevated, quasi-divine status of "God's beloved son." In the voice's affirmation that "with thee, I am well pleased," there is a distinct echo of the figure depicted in the book of Isaiah, "My chosen, in whom my soul delights" (Isa. 42:1). There the servant is described as someone on whom the spirit has been bestowed. He combines considerable physical weakness with a wondrous capacity for judgment:

Behold my servant, whom I uphold, my chosen, in whom my soul delights; I have put my spirit upon him, he will bring forth justice to the nations. He will not cry or lift up his voice; or make it heard in the street; a bruised reed he will not break, and a dimly burning wick he will not quench; he will faithfully bring forth justice. He will not fail or be discouraged till he has established justice in the earth; and the coastlands wait for his law. (42:1–4)

The combination of a quasi-divine glorification as the "son of God" with physical weakness and power of judgment is reminiscent of the figures in the Qumran documents that we have discussed earlier. Both the hero of the document in Aramaic and the hero of the self-glorification hymn combine glorification ("who is like me among the gods?") and a wonderful capacity for teaching and judgment ("no teaching is like my teaching") with weakness and suffering ("who is despised like me who is like me rejected of men").[7]

When Jesus finally entered Jerusalem with his followers, he took radical action. Entering the Temple courtyard, he drove out the buyers and sellers, including the pigeon vendors, and he over-turned the tables of the money-changers (Mark 11:15). Perhaps in this way Jesus sought to fulfill the concluding words of the book of Zechariah: "And there shall no longer be a Canaanite in the house of the Lord of hosts on that day" (Zech. 14:21). By "on that day," Zechariah would have meant the day of salvation. Jesus likely believed that traders and money-changers should not be in the house of the Lord of hosts on the day of salvation as well, but with one significant difference: Zechariah's timeline for the day of salvation was unknown, whereas for Jesus, it was happening in the here and now. In this regard, the word "Canaanite" can be understood not as a specific ethnic identity, but as a general name for traders, as is the case in Proverbs 31:24, where a wife is praised for delivering girdles to a Canaanite—that is, to a merchant. Thus we might read the verse in Zechariah as saying there shall no longer be a merchant in the house of the Lord on the day of salvation.

Whatever Jesus's rationale and scriptural support may have been, this action provoked commotion in the Temple and brought upon him the anger of the priests (Mark 11:18). Both the sale of animals to pilgrims and the acceptance of foreign money brought to the money-changers were then necessary to conduct the Temple rituals. People came from faraway countries to celebrate the festival in Jerusalem and to bring sacrifices to the Temple. They needed this marketplace to buy the animals required for their sacrifices, and if they did not have the local currency, they needed a money changer to get the local coins needed for the purchases.

But Jesus pronounced for all to hear that this activity was a desecration of the sanctity of the Temple, making it into a "den of thieves" (Mark 11:17). In effect, Jesus had chosen to create pandemonium in the most sensitive place—the courtyard of the Temple, the most holy place of the Jewish people; and at the most sensitive time—a few days before Passover, the festival that most of the Jews in the world wished to celebrate in the Temple since it was a symbol of unity and freedom.

About thirty years before these events, the great rebellion against the Romans had broken out just there during Passover. Three decades later, the members of the Roman garrison in the Antonia fortress overlooking the Temple undoubtedly would have observed Jesus's actions and been apprehensive about the consequences. From their point of view, Jesus was a successor of the messianic leaders of the great rebellion who had also laid claim to the throne (an event clearly recorded in Roman sources of that period). As such, they were convinced, Jesus wanted to take the same path as those other leaders. That is why at Jesus's crucifixion several days later the Romans would place a sign above the cross displaying the words "king of the Jews."

But a week before Passover, when Jesus cast out the vendors, overturned the tables, and decried the goings-on as having converted the Temple into a "den of thieves," neither the Roman authorities nor the priests arrested him. Why the Romans did not is unknown. The priests were too frightened to initiate such an arrest. Because many among the people hoped that he would prove to be the Messiah, son of David, who would redeem the people and restore their freedom, Jesus enjoyed much public sympathy among the Jews. His arrest at the Temple in the days before Passover was liable to stir a great commotion—a scenario the priests were determined to avoid (see Matt. 26:5; Mark 14:2). As a result, Jesus continued to go to the Temple courtyard every day in the week before Passover and speak about various religious issues.

A few days before his crucifixion, Jesus delivered a surprising sermon on the Messiah:

> How can the scribes say that the Messiah is the son of David? David himself, inspired by the Holy Spirit, declared, "The Lord said to my Lord, Sit at my right hand, till I put thy enemies under thy feet." David himself calls him Lord, so how is he his son? (Mark 12:35–37, and parallels, Matt. 22:42–45; Luke 20:41–44)

Jesus was referring to the opening verse of Psalm 110: "The Lord says to my Lord, Sit at my right hand, till I make your enemies your footstool." He was pointing out that according to this text, when David addresses the king-Messiah who is invited to sit on the right hand of God, David calls him "Lord." Then, Jesus commented, "David himself calls him Lord, so how is he his son?" In other words, if the Messiah was in fact from the house of David, David would have addressed him as "my son." With the support of this verse, Jesus was making an extraordinary claim: the Messiah described there, whose arrival the people was awaiting, was not a descendant of David!

Scholars have suggested that Jesus used this verse from the book of Psalms to show that although he did not descend genealogically from the house of David, he was the Messiah nevertheless.[8] If that was the case, this tradition concerning Jesus's sermon assumed that he did not belong to the house of David, which contradicts the contention of the gospels of Matthew and Luke that Jesus was in fact descended from this line (see Matt. 1:1; Luke 2:4). The very existence of this contradiction makes all the more likely the authenticity of the tradition that Jesus was not of the Davidic line and that he offered an extraordinary interpretation to support his claim to messiahship. It is hard to believe that New Testament authors would later *fabricate* a tradition opposed to the one in the gospels of Luke and Matthew.

And, in fact, in Jesus's own words, as related in the Gospels, he himself never claimed to be a descendant of the house of David. Some of the people around him did say that he was in the Davidic line—the beggar in Jericho called him "son of David," the people at the Mount of Olives pronounced "Blessed be the kingdom of our father David that is coming!" (Mark 10:46–48 and 11:10, and parallels)—but Jesus himself never confirmed it.

Yet there's more here. Jesus's sermon denying that the Messiah would be descended from the house of David also represented an ideological rejection of Davidic messianism, which expected the arrival of a fighting Messiah who would liberate the Jews from Roman rule. To Jesus, the Messiah was not cast in the mold of the warlike David, but was the son of God. As such, the Messiah was higher than David, which is why David had addressed him as "my Lord." The divine voice Jesus heard when he was baptized in the River Jordan had addressed him as "my son," and that is how he saw himself. Jesus would confirm this a few days later when he stood before the High Priest at his trial and asserted that he was "the Son of the Blessed one" (Mark 14:61–62).

Furthermore, as we said, as well as being the elevated "son of God," Jesus also saw himself in the image of Isaiah's suffering servant who atoned for the people through his sufferings and death. Jesus wished to sacrifice his life for this. Here, I agree with the doctor, philosopher, musician, theologian, and Nobel laureate

Albert Schweitzer, who proposed in his 1906 book, *The Quest of the Historical Jesus*,[9] that Jesus came to Jerusalem and created the disturbance in the Temple with the intention of being arrested and killed by the authorities. By sacrificing his life, Schweitzer argued, Jesus intended to set in motion the course of events that would bring about the kingdom of heaven on earth.

The Qumran writings, which it seems likely Jesus had encountered, further support this reading. Jesus saw himself as someone who would bring redemption and atonement to the world through his sufferings. The redemption he wished to achieve was not a political redemption effectuated through war, as many people at the time expected of a Messiah in the heroic warrior-Davidic tradition, but a spiritual redemption executed through suffering and a painful death. That is why the idea that the Messiah was not a descendant of the house of David was so important to Jesus. It rejected the hope of renewing the kingdom of Israel through military might like David's and made way for a different kind of Messiah—one whose mission was suffering, death, and atonement.

But it seems that this point was not understood by most of Jesus's disciples, who continued to hope that he would reveal himself as a warlike Messiah and a political redeemer. These disciples were consequently disappointed, and they—particularly Peter—would abandon him at the time of his trial and crucifixion. And as we discussed, the Romans would make a similar mistake about him, presuming that he aspired to be king of the Jews and their political redeemer. That is why they would place the sign "King of the Jews" above the cross.

At the same time, although the confrontation between Jesus and the Romans was political in nature, at Jesus's trial in the house of the High Priest the crux of the dispute was religious: the legitimacy of the messianic idea.

The Trial of Jesus

Pietà, mercy, the name of Michelangelo's famous 1499 sculpture in St. Peter's Basilica, depicts the dead Jesus lying in his mother's arms after he has been taken down from the cross. But this is a fictional scene.

As we saw, Jesus broke off relations with his family, including his mother, after being baptized by John the Baptist in the River Jordan. When he was crucified in Jerusalem, his family was not with him.[1] His break with his nuclear family was never healed in his lifetime—and, in fact, the substitute family he created for himself, his family of disciples, also collapsed at the time of his trial and crucifixion. Jesus's last words on the cross—"My God, my God, why hast thou forsaken me?" (Mark 15:34)–reflect his terrible loneliness at that moment.

It all began in the month of April, probably in the year 30 CE. Armed officers sent by the High Priest arrested Jesus at night, while he was praying in Gethsemane, an isolated place at the foot of the Mount of Olives. They took him to the house of the High Priest Joseph, son of Caiaphas, of the priestly house of Kathros, for trial. The Romans had granted this High Priest the authority to judge people who disturbed the order and rules in the Temple area.

That night, Caiaphas and his court questioned, judged, and condemned Jesus to death. They themselves, however, could not carry out the sentence, because the Romans denied Jewish courts of law the right to carry out death sentences. So court representatives delivered Jesus into the hands of the Roman governor Pontius Pilate the following morning. Upon receiving the prisoner Pilate confirmed the sentence of the Jewish court and ordered his soldiers to crucify him. Crucifixion was the standard Roman punishment for rebels. The Romans viewed Jesus as a rebel who sought to establish himself as "King of the Jews" (as attested by the sign they would affix near the cross: "Jesus of Nazareth King of the Jews").

On the surface, this is what happened to Jesus. But there is much more to say about how the trial of Jesus brought him to his death. The book-long journey we have undertaken to tease out the various competing Jewish approaches to the Messiah from the time of the Hebrew Bible on compels us to reconsider who Jesus's judges were and on what charge he was sentenced—and, ultimately, to reconceive why Jesus was crucified.

According to both Mark and Matthew, Jesus was taken on the night he was arrested to the house of the High Priest Caiaphas, where he was judged by the chief priests, the elders, and the scribes. Mark says: "And they led Jesus to the high priest and all the chief priests and the elders and the scribes were assembled" (Mark 14:53). Matthew explains: "Then, those who had seized Jesus led him to Caiaphas the high priest, where the scribes and the elders had gathered" (Matt. 26:57).

All of these priests were Sadducees. As we will see, none of the three synoptic gospels—Mark, Matthew, Luke—speak of the involvement of any Pharisees in the arrest and trial of Jesus. (The Greek word "synoptic" means, to be seen together. Since all three books share a common account, they can be read together.) While the gospel of John (which has a different story line) does mention Pharisees involved in Jesus's arrest (John 18:3), it seems that John is ahistorical at this point, and has an anti-Pharisee bias, given the multiple anti-Pharisee statements in the book. Also, John was written about 100 CE, furthest from the time of the depicted events. Mark was composed around 70 CE, Matthew around 85 CE, and Luke around 90 CE.

The Pharisees would have had no part in Jesus's trial because Jesus lived in the time when the Sadducees, headed by the High

Priest, were in charge of the Temple area. Furthermore, the trial took place at the High Priest's residence, where he was surrounded by his fellow Sadducee priests and the scribes who also worked in the Temple. Mixed Jewish courts of both Pharisee and Sadducee judges would rule on other occasions (to be discussed later in the chapter), but not at this time.

That said, can the synoptic gospel accounts of the trial before the High Priest be regarded as historical records? The scholar Paul Winter and judge Haim Cohen asserted that they could not.[2] These scholars pointed out the many contradictions between this trial as reported in Mark, Matthew, and Luke and the ordinances of the Pharisees and the sages as they are known to us from the Mishnah. According to the Mishnah, the president of the supreme court, not a High Priest, has to head the panel of judges. The trial was not held in the Chamber of Hewn Stones near the Temple— the only location, in mishnaic law, where any criminal proceeding with a possible death sentence could take place—but in the High Priest's residence. The trial was held at night, but according to the Mishnah, criminal cases were not tried at night. Moreover, Mark, Matthew, and Luke have the trial held on Passover night, but according to the Mishnah, trials were not to be convened on festivals. Again, the Mishnah prohibits sentencing the accused on his own evidence, but according to the synoptic gospels Jesus was sentenced on the basis of his own declarations in front of the High Priest:

> And they said: "what further testimony do we need? We have heard it ourselves from his own lips." (Luke 22:71)

Finally, the Mishnah stipulates that a blasphemer against God can be sentenced only if he pronounces God's ineffable name—

> The blasphemer is not culpable unless he pronounces the Name. (Sanh. 7:5)

—and Jesus did not do so. In his statements before the High Priest, Jesus used the epithet "Power" for God. Nevertheless he was sentenced as a blasphemer:

> And Jesus said: . . . and you will see the Son of man sitting at the right hand of Power . . . And the high priest tore his mantle and said: "why do we still need witnesses? You have heard his blasphemy." (Mark 14:62–64)

In response to these and similar assertions, the German scholar Joseph Blinzeler ably countered that because Jesus's judges were Sadducees and not Pharisees, the trial cannot be understood in the context of the laws of the Mishnah, which were based on the Pharisee tradition.[3] The trial would have proceeded according to Sadducee law, which was principally based on the Bible. Thus, for example, the fact that Jesus was sentenced on the basis of his own statements was in accordance with biblical precedents such as Joshua 7:19–20 and 2 Samuel 1:16. As the book of Joshua reports:

> Then Joshua said to Achan, "My son, pay honor to the Lord, the God of Israel, and make confessions to Him. Tell me what you have done; do not hold anything back from me." Achan answered Joshua, "It is true, I have sinned against the Lord, the God of Israel. This is what I did." (Josh. 7:19–20)

And soon after this confession,

> Joshua said, "What calamity you have brought upon us! The Lord will bring calamity upon you this day." And all Israel pelted him with stones. They put him to the fire and stoned them. (Josh. 7:25)

The Bible says nothing about who should conduct a trial or on what days or times it should take place. Thus the Sadducees' trial of Jesus was in keeping with biblical precedent to the extent that it existed. Jesus's death sentence for blasphemy against God was also in keeping with non-Pharisaic writings of the Second Temple period, in which blasphemy was not restricted to uttering the ineffable name of God. As the New Testament scholar Adela Yarbro-Collins observed, Philo of Alexandria, a contemporary of Jesus who was not affiliated with any of the sects, held that any man who claimed for himself a divine status, as Jesus did, was a blasphemer against God.[4]

How, then, did Jesus come to be accused of blasphemy? As we saw, in the days before his trial, in his sermon in the Temple, Jesus had proclaimed that the Messiah was not the son of David. The Gospels relate that before Jesus made this assertion, he engaged in a dispute with some Sadducees:

> Then the Sadducees, who say there is no resurrection, came to him with a question. "Teacher," they said, "Moses wrote for us that if a man's brother dies and leaves a wife but no children, the man must marry the widow and raise up offspring for his brother. Now there were seven brothers. The first one married and died without leaving any children. The second one married the widow, but he also died, leaving no child. It was the same with the third. In fact, none of the seven left any children. Last of all, the woman died too. At the resurrection whose wife will she be, since the seven were married to her?" Jesus replied, "Are you not in error because you do not know the Scriptures or the power of God?" (Mark 12:18–24; see also Matt. 22:23–33; Luke 20:27–40)

Jesus then retorted that the Sadducees were greatly mistaken in not believing in resurrection:

> "As for the dead being raised, have you not read in the book of Moses, in the passage about the bush, how God spoke to

him, saying, 'I am the God of Abraham, and the God of Isaac, and the God of Jacob'? He is not God of the dead, but of the living. You are quite wrong." (Mark 12:26–27)

A little later, when Jesus was teaching in the Temple courts, he made the assertion that the Messiah was *not* the son of David, asking:

How can the scribes say that the Messiah is the son of David? David himself, inspired by the Holy Spirit, declared, "The Lord said to my Lord, Sit at my right hand, till I put thy enemies under thy feet." David himself calls him Lord, so how is he his son? (Mark 12:35–37).

In view of the closeness of both of these happenings, on the same day, within the Temple court, it seems likely that the Sadducees also heard Jesus claim that the Messiah was not the son of David.

As we've pointed out, Jesus's controversial assertion about the provenance of the Messiah was based on Psalm 110. As we have seen, an earlier formulation of Psalms 110:3, reflected in the Septuagint, describes the king as someone born by God "from the womb of the morning." As such, the Sadducees and scribes who would have been familiar with these texts could well have determined that Jesus was telling them: *The Messiah is not a descendant of the house of David. He has a higher status than David, and that is why David calls him "my Lord" at the beginning of the psalm. The Messiah is higher than David because he is the son of God and was born from the womb of the morning.*

Because Jesus was tried by priests who were Sadducees and scribes, it is reasonable to suppose that some of them were among the Sadducees and scribes who heard Jesus in the Temple. They may have told the High Priest that Jesus had said the Messiah was higher than David and that he was the son of God.

As we have discussed, the Sadducees, who also included the High Priest, opposed the idea of a Messiah in general, and especially the idea that the Messiah was the son of God. To them, these concepts amounted to blasphemy against God. The supposed existence of a semidivine figure (sometimes identified in the Psalms and the writings of the prophets as God's son) was fully at odds with their fidelity to the Torah's insistence on maintaining a clear distinction between the human and the divine. Furthermore, the claim about the King-Messiah as "Son of God" subordinated God to the biological cycles of birth, sexuality, and fertility.

This may have been the background to the first question the High Priest put to Jesus in the trial:

"Are you the Messiah, the son of the Blessed One?" (Mark 14:61)

That is, do you see yourself as the son of God? The High Priest's choice of the term "the Blessed One," a common expression for God in the Jewish sources of the period, was deliberate. He thus avoided using the expression "the son of God" himself.

Jesus answered the High Priest's question:

I am, and you will see the son of man sitting at the right hand of Power, and coming with the clouds of heaven. (Mark 14:62)

Just as the High Priest used the expression "the Blessed One" for God, Jesus used another accepted expression, "Power." That this dialogue includes the use of various expressions for God common at that period gives credence to its being an authentic record of the exchange between the High Priest and Jesus.

Jesus's answer is clearly based on two passages from Scripture. In the first verse of Psalm 110, God says to a king, "Sit at my right hand, till I make your enemies your footstool"; and Daniel describes the "son of man" as coming with the clouds of heaven:

As I looked on, in the night vision,
one like a son of man

came with the clouds of heaven. (Dan. 7:13)

At the same time, Jesus's statement about the son of God sitting in heaven also recalls the self-glorification in the Qumran hymn, in which the speaker claimed to have sat in heaven "on a mighty throne in the angelic councils" (see chapter 9). These textual allusions show that Jesus believed the Messiah had a quasi-divine status.

After Jesus declared that he saw himself as the son of God, the High Priest rent his garments, as biblical law required upon hearing words of blasphemy against God (see, for instance, 2 Kings 18:37; 19:1). Mark relates:

> Then the high priest tore his clothing and said, "Why do we need other witnesses?" (Mark 14:63)

The High Priest called upon the chief priests, elders, and scribes beside him for their decision:

> You have all heard his blasphemy. "What is your decision?" and they all condemned him as deserving death. (Mark 14:64)

The High Priest and the other judges condemned Jesus to death in accordance with the biblical law concerning blasphemy:

> "Take the blasphemer outside the camp, and let all who were within hearing lay their hands upon his head, and let the whole community stone him." (Lev. 24:14; also see 1 Kings 21:10).

The trial ended in the condemnation to death mentioned in Mark 14:64.

The next morning, Sadducee representatives delivered Jesus to the Roman governor, Pontius Pilate. Pilate first questioned Jesus, "Are you the King of the Jews?" Jesus responded, "You have said so" (Mark 15:2). Then the chief priests in attendance voiced many accusations against Jesus, who stayed silent. Even when Pilate asked Jesus, "Aren't you going to answer?," Jesus did not reply (15:3–5).

Then Pilate ordered that Jesus be crucified.[5] The Roman soldiers carried out the sentence, crucifying Jesus outside of the wall of Jerusalem in front of a Jewish crowd. Misunderstanding his intentions, above the cross the soldiers placed the sign, "King of the Jews."

Like the Romans, the general populace did not understand Jesus's concept of messiahship. Until his trial, the Jews expected Jesus to reveal himself as a belligerent Messiah who would redeem the people of Israel politically and militarily. They liked him, acclaimed him, and supported him (Mark 11:8–10; 12:37; 14:2). But after the trial, when their hopes were dashed, many among the people turned against him.

Something similar happened among his disciples. When Jesus told them of the mystery of the suffering Messiah who atoned for the sins of humankind, they did not understand or absorb it, and continued to expect that Jesus would reveal himself as the political redeemer of the people of Israel. After his trial, they distanced themselves from him, out of disappointment and probably self-preservation. Even Peter, his most faithful, denied being Jesus's disciple three times on the night of the crucifixion. When a servant girl of the High Priest said to Peter, "You were one of those with Jesus of Nazareth," he responded, "I don't know what you're talking about." When she held her ground, telling others nearby, "This man is definitely one of them," Peter continued to protest: "I do not know this man of whom you speak!" But the bystanders said to Peter, "Certainly you are one of them, for you are a Galilean" (Mark 14:67–71).

Jesus's other disciples also abandoned him: "Then all his disciples deserted him and ran away" (Mark 14:50).[6] When Jesus died on the cross, none of his disciples or his family were with him. Only a group of faithful women who had come with him from Galilee observed the crucifixion from afar (Mark 15:40–41). (John 19:26 does say that Jesus's mother and the disciple he loved were next to the cross, but most scholars view this statement as a later addition and unreliable.) Later, Jesus rebuked his disciples for their disbelief (Mark 16:14).

As we saw, the synoptic gospels only discuss the trial of Jesus in the context of the Sadducee priests and the scribes. Apparently because the trial took place at night at the High Priest's residence, and not in the locus of the official court, only the Sadducee priests and the scribes were present. The Pharisees could not have been present for this trial, as it contravened their law. The trial was held at night, possibly on a holiday, and in the High Priest's house, rather than in an acceptable place near the Temple.

Even if the Pharisees had participated in the trial, *they would not have condemned Jesus to death.* The Sadducees condemned Jesus to death on the charge of blasphemy—that is, in accordance with their understanding of what constituted blasphemy. The Pharisees would not have deemed Jesus blasphemous for attributing a semidivine status to himself, because they, too, believed that a semidivine Messiah would be coming to deliver them from Roman rule. This is why the Pharisaic Psalms of Solomon could proclaim:

> See, O Lord, and raise up for them their king,
> the son of David,
> at the time which you chose, O God,
> to rule over Israel your servant.
> And gird him with strength to shatter
>   in pieces unrighteous rulers,
> to purify Jerusalem from nations that trample
>   her down in destruction. . . .
> And he shall be a righteous king,
> taught by God, over them,
> and there shall be no injustice in his days in their midst,
> for all shall be holy, and their king the Lord-
>   Messiah. (Ps. of Solomon 17:21–22,32)

Most importantly, as we saw, the Pharisees believed that a blasphemer had to utter the unutterable name of God—"The blasphemer is not culpable unless he pronounces the Name" (Sanh. 7:5)—and Jesus never did so at the trial; he solely referred to himself in relation to the "Power," an acceptable expression of that period.

In essence, it now appears, the trial of Jesus was the culmination of a 750-year conflict between two different biblical currents regarding the Messiah. The confrontation between Jesus and his judges was an outgrowth of two schools of thought that had existed concurrently in the Jewish tradition since the preaching of the prophets Isaiah and Hosea, a controversy with tragic consequences.

The Sadducee priests adopted the position found in the priestly sections of the Torah that sought to glorify God and create a clear distinction between the human and the divine. Since the divine was above the biological dimension of created nature, God could have nothing to do with sexuality or birth. It was thus inconceivable that God could have a son. From the Sadducee point of view, Jesus's claim that he was the son of God was such blasphemy and desecration that one had to rend one's garments on hearing it. The punishment for such a blasphemer was death.

Against this, Jesus based his claim to messiahship on psalms that glorified the king-Messiah ("You are the fairest of the sons of man, grace is poured upon your lips, therefore God has blessed you forever," Ps. 45:2); declared such a one to be the son of God ("You are my son, today I have begotten you," Ps. 2:7); and predicted that he was destined to sit beside God in heaven ("Sit at my right hand, till I make your enemies your footstool," Ps. 110:1).

The Pharisees agreed with all of these ideas from Psalms. In their view, a king-Messiah of the house of David would arrive to crush "unrighteous rulers" and cleanse Jerusalem from the nations that had trampled it underfoot:

See, O Lord, and raise up for them their king,
the son of David,
at the time which you chose, O God,
to rule over Israel your servant.
And gird him with strength to shatter
   in pieces unrighteous rulers,
to purify Jerusalem from nations that trample her
   down in destruction. (Ps. of Solomon 17:21–22)

Jesus may also have been exposed to and influenced by Qumran ideology. As we saw, three Qumran texts present the idea of an unusual messianic or priestly leader who is exalted with a quasi-divine status ("Who is like me among the gods?"); who suffers ("your blood . . . the blows of your pain"); and who atones by his suffering ("atoned for all the members of his generation").[7] In fact, of all the major groups active at the end of the Second Temple period, the Sadducees were the only group to deny the idea of a Messiah. Messianism was present in the ideas of the Pharisees, the writings of the Qumran sect, and of course in the Christian view.

The essential agreement between the Pharisees and Jesus and his disciples, and their mutual opposition to the Sadducees, can be seen in other ways in the period following Jesus's crucifixion. The historian Josephus Flavius points to a split between the Sadducees and Pharisees in relation to the killing of Jesus's brother James. Josephus identifies the Sadducee High Priest, Hanan ben Hanan as the killer, and adds that some people who were "strict in the observance of the law"—that is, the Pharisees—disapproved of the killing.[8]

A few years after Jesus's trial, some of his disciples were put on trial for following Christianity. Unlike the court that had judged Jesus, which as we know was composed entirely of Sadducees, his disciples stood before a mixed court comprising both Sadducees and Pharisees. While the Sadducees demonstrated a very hostile attitude to Jesus's disciples, as they had toward Jesus himself, the Pharisees supported the disciples to a greater or lesser degree.

Here we must draw particular attention to the figures of Rabbi Gamliel the Elder, the grandson of Hillel the Elder, and Gamliel's student, the Apostle Paul. Although Rabbi Gamliel did not give Jesus's disciples his full support, he stood by them and defended them at the trial. He opposed the persecution of messianic movements in general (Acts 5:34). Gamaliel's pupil, the Apostle Paul, persecuted the Christians at the beginning of his career, but not on behalf of his Pharisee teacher. Instead, he was equipped with letters from the Sadducee High Priest and his council of elders: "And I persecuted the followers of the Way, hounding some to death, arresting both men and women and throwing them in prison. The high priest and the whole council of elders can testify that this is so. For I received letters from them to our Jewish brothers in Damascus, authorizing me to bring the followers of the Way from there to Jerusalem, in chains, to be punished" (Acts 22:4–5).

Moreover, when Paul left the Pharisees, began to follow the path of Jesus, and was put on trial before the Sanhedrin as a result, the Pharisees nonetheless intervened on his behalf on account of their similar views on the question of the resurrection of the dead:

Paul realized that some members of the high council were Sadducees and some were Pharisees, so he shouted, "Brothers, I am a Pharisee, as were my ancestors! And I am on trial because my hope is in the resurrection of the dead!." This divided the council—the Pharisees against the Sadducees—for the Sadducees say there is no resurrection or angels or spirits, but the Pharisees believe in all of these. So there was a great uproar. Some of the teachers of religious law who were Pharisees jumped up and began to argue forcefully. "We see nothing wrong with him," they shouted. "Perhaps a spirit or an angel spoke to him." (Acts 23:6–9)

Forty years after Jesus's trial and his crucifixion by the Romans, the Romans laid waste to Jerusalem and the Temple. Many of the Sadducee priests perished in the flames that engulfed the Temple;

others were taken to Rome and sold as slaves. It can be said that in 70 CE, with the destruction of the Temple, the Sadducees disappeared from history and ceased to exist as a Jewish group. The leadership of the people passed to the sages, the Rabbis, who were the heirs and successors of the Pharisees.

Like the Pharisees, the sages also believed in the appearance of a Messiah of a quasi-divine nature.[9] Rabbi Akiva, one of the greatest sages of the Tannaim (authorities quoted in the Mishnah), claimed that one of the thrones set up in heaven, described in the book of Daniel, be given to God and that the other be given to David (*b.Hagiga* 14a). Rabbi Akiva also supported the messianic leader Bar Kokhba, according him a celestial status by connecting him with the verse "there shall come a star [*kokhav*] out of Jacob" (*y.Tanit* 4:8 [68d]).

It seems clear that these sages, and especially Rabbi Akiva, would not have sentenced Jesus to death for his messianic views, which were not so different from their own. But owing to tragic historical circumstances, Jesus lived in the time when the Sadducees were in charge of the Temple, and he was judged by them.

It is a great distortion of history to place the blame for Jesus's crucifixion on the Jewish people as a whole. Ultimately the Roman governor Pontius Pilate delivered the death sentence, and Roman soldiers carried out the crucifixion. Moreover, according to all the evidence, the Sadducees who initially condemned Jesus to death were in the minority of the Jewish people. Most people in Jesus's period supported the Pharisees, who, like Jesus and his disciples, believed in the appearance of a Messiah of a divine nature (as well as the resurrection of the dead). Furthermore, historical Judaism, which developed after the Second Temple's destruction under the Rabbis' leadership, also accepted the hope of a Messiah of a superhuman kind. On the question of Jesus's messianic conception and that of historical Judaism, there is essential agreement even though Jews do not accept Jesus as the Messiah. The Jewish people supported, and a great many Jews today still support, the hope of a Messiah. Jesus's judges belonged to a small antimessianic group, the Sadducees, which one generation after Jesus disappeared from history.

The great split between Judaism and Christianity did not take place in the time of Jesus, but later, following the actions of Paul, who was not a personal acquaintance of Jesus and not one of his disciples. Paul essentially annulled the obligation to observe the commandments, producing a great rift between Christianity and historical Judaism, which was rooted in the commandments. But this action of Paul's was not connected with the historical Jesus, who observed the commandments and, as he himself said, had no desire to annul even one of them. (Matt. 5:17–20).

Today, after many hundreds of years of hostility between Christians and the Jewish people, who have been unjustly blamed for the crucifixion of Jesus, this reexamination of the history of the messianic idea permits us to see the trial of Jesus in its broader and deeper social and ideological context. The trial of Jesus was *not* a clash of Jewish and Christian doctrines, but a confrontation between two internal Jewish positions—of expecting a Messiah or rejecting the messianic idea—in which Jesus and the Pharisees were on the same side. The Pharisees did disagree with Jesus principally about whether Jesus himself was the Messiah—but historically, for Jews, arguing about who was or wasn't the Messiah was nothing out of the ordinary. The Pharisees did not condemn the pretenders mentioned by Gamliel in Acts 5:34–38 and various others.

One could even say that Jesus's trial arose almost by accident. Had the Romans granted the Pharisees rather than the Sadducees the authority to judge people who disturbed the order and rules in the Temple area, and had Jesus's judges been Pharisees rather than Sadducees, Jesus would not have been condemned to death, convicted, and crucified.

It is my hope that this work will give rise to new discourse, understanding, and healing between Jews and Christians.

Afterword

The central focus of this book has been the Jewish dispute regarding messianism. On the one hand, there is the monarchic-messianic ideology that elevates the king to a semidivine status, grants him divine names, describes him as the "son of God," and ascribes to him eternal life. On the other hand, there is the antimessianic movement, which dismisses the possibility that a flesh-and-blood king can ascend to a semidivine status. According to this way of thinking, there is a sharp divide between the divine and the human realms, and ideology must respect it. God does not sire children, and a human king does not have eternal life.

Despite these disagreements, early on in the creation of the Hebrew Bible there was general consensus among all the authors that God transcended suffering. God could not suffer; only humanity suffered. The verbs that designated physical suffering were never applied to God. Similarly, the monarchic-messianic school that saw the king as a quasi-divine being also dismissed the possibility of a suffering messiah-king.

When Second Isaiah focused his prophecy on the suffering servant, this figure was not messianic:

> He was despised, shunned by men,
> A man of suffering, familiar with disease
> As one who hid his face from us. . . .
> Yet it was our sickness that he was bearing
> Our suffering that he endured. (Isa. 53:3–5)

What is more, Second Isaiah identifies Cyrus, king of Persia, as

God's emissary, who will do God's will through his promise to build the Temple in Jerusalem:

> [The Lord] says of Cyrus,
> "He is my shepherd,
> and he shall fulfill all my purpose";
> saying of Jerusalem, "She shall be built,"
> and of the temple, "Your foundation
>   shall be laid." (Isa. 44:28)

Second Isaiah's Messiah is the triumphant King Cyrus of Persia, and the grace granted to David is now given to all Israel. Thus in the original text of the Hebrew Bible there is no place for a suffering God or a suffering Messiah.

And yet, following a textual change in Isaiah 63:9, which took place at a fairly early date, before the canonization of the prophetic books, a different picture is painted. As a result of this textual change, we now read in the book of Isaiah the following words:

> In all their troubles He was troubled [לֹו צַר],
> And the angel of His Presence delivered them.
> In His love and pity He Himself redeemed them,
> Raised them, and exalted them All
>   the days of old. (Isa. 63:9)

Written in this way, the verse claims that God was troubled and suffered together with the people of Israel. However, this is not the original version of this verse. In the original version, reflected in the ancient Greek translation—the Septuagint—as well as in the Isaiah scroll of Qumran and the Ketib tradition of the Masoretic text, the second Hebrew word in that second clause is the word of negation, "lo" (לֹא), meaning "no." This changes the punctuation of the verse, which we need to understand thusly: "In all their troubles it was not an emissary [צִיר לֹא], or an angel. His Presence delivered them."

This version is making a strong statement: that God, and not an angel or an emissary, redeemed the Israelites from their hardship. This is akin to what it says in the Passover Haggadah: "I, and not an angel . . . I and not a seraph . . . I and not an emissary . . . I my self and not anyone else [delivered Israel from Egypt]." The words "His Presence delivered them" may be understood in the context of Deuteronomy 4:37: "He took you out from Egypt through His presence and His great might." In other words, God Himself—*His* presence—saved and redeemed the Israelites. According to this original reading there is nothing in this verse to attest the idea that God suffers with the people of Israel.

The slight textual change from the word "lo'" (לא) (no) to the prepositional "lo" (לו), meaning "to him" or "for him," which produced a very different meaning, is the first insertion of the idea of a suffering God into the Hebrew Bible. Such an idea had been foreign to biblical thinking, but the person who modified the verse wished to incorporate this ideological innovation into the Bible.

When was this verse modified? One cannot be certain, but one may offer a terminus ad quem, a latest date possible.

We can make the assessment based on another development in this text: the first appearance of an unknown angelic figure. The emended version of Isaiah 63:9 speaks of "the angel of His Presence," meaning that God has designated a specific angel as such: that angel who is in the immediate presence of God. God has sent this angel to redeem the Israelites. Postbiblical Jewish literature refers to "the angel of Presence" multiple times. Yehoel or Metatron, as the angel is named in the literature, is understood to be particularly close to God and to see God's countenance.

According to the book of Jubilees, a sectarian work created in circles ideologically adjacent to the Qumran sect (fragments of Jubilees were found among the Dead Sea scrolls), the angel of the Presence dictated the contents of Jubilees to Moses when the latter ascended to Mount Sinai:

> And He said to the angel of the presence: "Write for Moses from the beginning of creation till My sanctuary has been built among them for all eternity." (Jub. 1:27)

The author of Jubilees was thus familiar with the emended version of Isaiah 63:9, since it had to have been from there that he drew the figure of the angel of the Presence. The book of Jubilees was likely composed toward the end of the second century BCE, and so it stands to reason that the emendation of Isaiah 63:9 occurred before that date.[1]

From the moment the biblical God was depicted as saddened and suffering with God's own people, the door was opened to the depiction of a Messiah who occupied a quasi-divine stature and was also sad and suffering. This is the figure of the protagonist of the self-glorification hymn from Qumran. As was mentioned, the hymn describes this figure as sitting on a splendid throne in the heavens. On the one hand, the hero of the hymn exclaims, "Who is like me among the gods?" On the other hand, he suffers afflictions, and proclaims "Who is disgraced like I am?"[2]

These are important links in the chains connecting the quasi-divine messianic figure with suffering and affliction. At first the God of the Hebrew Bible was not shown to suffer, and the idealized biblical messiah was depicted as transcending suffering as well. Second Isaiah created the nonmessianic figure of the suffering servant. The emendation producing "in all their troubles He was troubled" created a bold and even revolutionary depiction of a God who suffered together with God's people and the angel of the Presence—this portrayal appearing as early as the second-century book of Jubilees.

Thus the image of a God who suffers together with God's people was extant in Jewish tradition prior to the birth of Christianity. From the moment that the idea of a saddened God suffering with God's people was accepted, one could also attribute the same suffering to the quasi-divine messianic figure. We see this attribution in a number of the Dead Sea scrolls, in early Christian texts, and in rabbinic literature.

This is yet another example of how Jewish and Christian images of the Messiah were very similar to one another. It is only the tragic circumstance of history that put the trial of Jesus in the hands of a minority and unrepresentative faction of a community otherwise sharing similar messianic conceptions.

Notes

I. BIRTH OF THE MESSIANIC FIGURE

1. Y.Berakhot 2:4 (5a).
2. See, for an example of this symbol, Isaiah 10:5.
3. See a summary of the scholarship on this possibility in Roberts, "Whose Child Is This?"
4. Begrich, "Jesaja 14, 28–32," 121–31.
5. Childs, *Isaiah*, 80.
6. Kaufmann, *History of Israelite Religion*, 648–50.
7. In Inbar, *Prophecies, Pacts, and Tribes*, 66.

2. REJECTION OF THE KINGSHIP CONCEPT

1. Apart from his having lived in the Northern Kingdom of Israel, we know very little about Hosea's life. We do not know, for example, what town he lived in, or what happened to him when the Assyrians conquered the country. Perhaps he was exiled; perhaps he escaped to Jerusalem like other refugees from the kingdom of Israel, and took his prophecies there; or perhaps he remained behind with the poor people in the north.
2. In the version reflected in the Septuagint translation of Hosea 4:2 the word "pillar" was changed to "altar," "ephod" to "priesthood," and "teraphim" to "urim" (sacred mantic stones). This version is likely the product of the book's redactors in Jerusalem, who were supportive of the monarchic regime, as we've noted. As opposed to Hosea, who was against the monarchy, these editors wished to legitimize the king, and to that end they removed the forbidden and derided cultic elements mentioned in this verse since these were adjacent to references to the king. Instead of these forbidden elements they substituted acceptable cultic elements and concepts— namely, the altar, priesthood, and *urim*.
3. See Deut. 16:22. The prohibition of the pillar comes together with

the prohibition of the Ashera tree. Both were part of the popular cult that Deuteronomy rejected.

4. See Macintosh, *Hosea*, 539–40.
5. See Hosea 2:16–17, 9:10, and compare Jer. 2:2. Regarding the Sin of Baal Pe'or, see Num. 25:1–5.
6. Wellhausen, *Die kleinen Propheten*, 134.
7. See a summary of scholarship on this matter in Weinfeld, *Deuteronomy 1–11*, 44–57.
8. Ginsberg, *Israelian Heritage of Judaism*, 23–24.

3. RECONCEIVING THE MESSIAH

1. Williamson, *Book Called Isaiah*.
2. See Ezra 1:1–4, 6:3–5; 2 Chron. 36:23.

4. MESSIANIC RISE AND FALL

1. Fleming, *Installation of Baal's High Priestess*.
2. See, for example, 1 Sam. 4:4, 14:3, 22:10, 23:6–12; 2 Sam. 5:19, 11:11.
3. Kaufmann, *History of Israelite Religion*, 4, 242.

5. SHIFTING SANDS OF TORAH AUTHORITY

1. See Knohl, *Sanctuary of Silence*, 101–3; see also Milgrom, *Leviticus 17–22, AB*, 1332–45.

6. THE HUMAN AND THE DIVINE

1. Loewenstamm, "Death of Moses," 142–47.
2. The J source, or the Yahwist, is the source that uses the divine name YHWH already in the book of Genesis. Other sources avoid the use of this name in Genesis since they think that it was first revealed in the time of Moses.
3. Kaufmann, *History of Israelite Religion*, 60–63.
4. Roberts, "What Child Is This?"
5. Tigay, "Divine Creation of the King in Psalms 2:6."
6. Breasted, *Ancient Records of Egypt*, vol. 2, 75–100, 334; vol. 3, 12–19; Gardiner, "Coronation of King Hamerhab."
7. Regarding sitting next to the king as a gesture of respect, see 1 Kings 2:19.
8. Kaufmann, *History of Israelite Religion*, 60–63.

7. INTRODUCING RESURRECTION

1. According to the Rabbis, the official end of prophecy was in the Persian period, after the time of Haggai, Zechariah, and Malachi (see b. Sanhedrin 11a). Daniel is the latest book in the Hebrew Bible. It is the only book written in the Hellenistic period.

2. The book of Daniel is clearly divided into two parts. In the first part, chapters 1–6, Daniel is represented as an eminent sage who interprets the dreams of the foreign rulers of his day. In the second part, Daniel himself has visions, but he is unable to interpret them, so a heavenly being, a kind of angel, explains his visions to him. There is some controversy concerning the time of writing of the first part and the author's identity (was it really written by someone living at the time of Antiochus's edicts of religious persecution?), but these matters are beyond the purview of this volume.

3. See, for example, Ps. 88:11; Job 7:9–10.

8. THE SADDUCEES' DENIAL

1. *Avot DeRabi Natan*, version A, Shechter edition, 26.
2. *Avot DeRabi Natan*, version A, Shechter edition, 26.
3. Midrash Bereshit Rabba 65, Theodore-Albeck edition, 742.
4. Josephus, *Jewish Wars*, 2:164–65, translated by H. J. Thackeray, 387.
5. Knohl, *Sanctuary of Silence*, 137–64. See also Knohl, *Divine Symphony*, 28–35.
6. Olyan, *Violent Rituals of the Hebrew Bible*, 122.

9. QUMRAN ACCOUNTS

1. The present author and Prof. Sh. Talmon published several fragments of the Qumran calendar. See for instance Talmon and Knohl, "A Calendrical Scroll."
2. See Qimron and Strugnell, Miqsat Maʿase Ha-Torah, 27.
3. Sievers, "Josephus, First Maccabees, Sparta, the Three Haireseis— and Cicero."
4. The sectarian writings must be distinguished from biblical texts and other nonsectarian texts found at Qumran, some of which may not have been written by the sect itself, and may have been brought at an earlier time by the people of Qumran to their settlement.
5. Flusser, *Judaism of the Second Temple Period*, 333.

6. 4Q252, col. 5, in Martinez and Tigchelaar, *Dead Sea Scrolls*, vol. 1, 504.

7. 4Q174, frg. 1, line 10, in Martinez and Tigchelaar, *Dead Sea Scrolls*, vol. 1, 352.

8. Talmon, "Waiting for the Messiah at Qumran."

9. 1Qsb, V, 26–29, in Martinez and Tigchelaar, *Dead Sea Scrolls*, vol. 1, 108.

10. Kutscher, *Language and the Linguistic Background*, 197.

11. 4Q541, frg. 9, lines 3–4, in Martinez and Tigchelaar, *Dead Sea Scrolls*, vol. 2, 1080.

12. 1Qsb, IV, 27, in Martinez and Tigchelaar, *Dead Sea Scrolls*, vol. 1, 106.

13. 4Q541, frg. 4, line 3, in Martinez and Tigchelaar, *Dead Sea Scrolls*, vol. 2, 1078.

14. 4Q541, frg. 9, line 6, in Martinez and Tigchelaar, *Dead Sea Scrolls*, vol. 2, 1080.

15. 4Q541, frg. 9, line 2, in Martinez and Tigchelaar, *Dead Sea Scrolls*, vol. 2, 1080.

16. J. Baumgarten, "Messianic Forgiveness of Sin."

17. Greenberg, "Cities of Asylum," 386.

18. Knohl, *Messiah before Jesus*, 1–26, 75–86.

19. See Eshel, "4Q Self-Glorification Hymn," 428, line 5.

20. 4Q491, frg. 11a, line 6, in Martinez and Tigchelaar, *Dead Sea Scrolls*, vol. 2, 980.

21. 4Q491, frg. 11a, line 2, in Martinez and Tigchelaar, *Dead Sea Scrolls*, vol. 2, 980.

22. 4Q491, frg. 11a, line 9, in Martinez and Tigchelaar, *Dead Sea Scrolls*, vol. 2, 980.

23. See Schuller, "4Q427," col. 2, p. 97.

10. THE PHARISEES' EXPECTATIONS

1. See the sources and discussion in Knohl, *Divine Symphony*, 127–32.

2. Josephus, *Jewish Antiquities* 13:288–98; and compare *b. Kiddushin* 66a.

3. Joosten, "Reflections on the Original Language."

4. Moshe Zeidel makes this point in "Parallels between the Books of Isaiah and Psalms."

5. Klausner, *Messianic Idea in Israel*, 321n10.

6. Bird, Are You the One Who Is to Come?, 54; Wright, "Psalms of Solomon," 667–68.

11. JESUS'S MESSIANIC CONCEPTION

1. Wrede, *Messianic Secret*, translated by J. C. G. Grieg.
2. 4Q541, frg. 4, line 3 in Martinez and Tigchelaar, *Dead Sea Scrolls*, vol. 2.
3. 4Q541, frg. 9, line 6 in Martinez and Tigchelaar, *Dead Sea Scrolls*, vol. 2.
4. 4Q541, frg. 9, line 2 in Martinez and Tigchelaar, *Dead Sea Scrolls*, vol. 2.
5. Flusser, *Judaism and the Origins of Christianity*, 143–44.
6. Flusser, *Judaism and the Origins of Christianity*, 141–49.
7. 4Q541; 4Q471b in Martinez and Tigchelaar, *Dead Sea Scrolls*, vol. 2.
8. See Fredriksen, *Jesus of Nazareth, King of the Jews*, 141.
9. Schweitzer, *Quest of the Historical Jesus*.

12. THE TRIAL OF JESUS

1. This is confirmed by the account of all the synoptic gospels. See Yarbro-Collins, *Mark, Hermeneia*, 774–75. The story in John 19:26–27 about the presence of Jesus's mother at the cross is late and ahistorical.
2. Winter, *On the Trial of Jesus*, 31–43; Cohen, *Trial and Death of Jesus*, 86–96.
3. Blinzeler, "Das Synedrium von Jerusalem und die Strafprozessordnung der Mischna," 54–65.
4. Yarbro-Collins, "Charge of Blasphemy in Mark 14.64."
5. Mark also relates that Pilate asked the Jewish people who had gathered there about what should be done with Jesus, and the crowd called for his crucifixion. However, scholars suspect that this narrative is not historical and was added with the intent to blame the entire Jewish people for the death of Jesus. See Sanders, *Jesus and Judaism*, 298.
6. For justification of this translation see Yarbro-Collins, *Mark, Hermeneia*, 687.
7. See Eshel, "4Q Self-Glorification Hymn," 428, line 5; 4Q541, frg. 4, line 3; 4Q541, frg. 9, line 2.
8. Josephus, *Jewish Antiquities*, 20, 198–203.
9. The Pharisees and the Rabbis also believed in the resurrection of the dead and included a reference to it in the *Amidah* prayer: "Blessed are you God who resurrects the dead."

AFTERWORD

1. Questions regarding the unity of the book of Jubilees, the way it was written, and its date are not easily addressed. On all three issues see Segal, *Book of Jubilees*. Also regarding the date, see Werman, *Book of Jubilees*, 45–48.
2. Eshel, "4Q Self-Glorification Hymn," 428.

Bibliography

Anbar, Moshe. *Prophecy, Treaty-Making, and Tribes in the Mary Documents.* [In Hebrew.] Jerusalem: Bialik Institute, 2007.

Baumgarten, Joseph M. "Messianic Forgiveness of Sin in CD 14:9 (4Q266 10i 12–13)." In *The Provo International Conference on the Dead Sea Scrolls,* edited by D. W. Parry and E. Ulrich, 537–44. Leiden: Brill, 1999.

Begrich, Joachim. "Jesaja 14, 28–32." [In German.] *Zeitschrift der Deutschen Morgen Ländischen Gesellschaft* 1 (1933): 121–31.

Bird, Michael F. *Are You the One Who Is to Come?* Grand Rapids MI: Baker Academic, 2009.

Blinzeler, Joseph. "Das Synedrium von Jerusalem und die Strafprozessordnung der Mischna." [In German.] *ZNW* 52 (1961): 4–65.

Breasted, James H. *Ancient Records of Egypt.* 5 vols. Chicago: University of Chicago Press, 1906–7.

Childs, Brevard S. *Isaiah: A Commentary.* Old Testament Library. Louisville KY: Westminster John Knox, 2001.

Cohen, Haim Hermann. *The Trial and Death of Jesus.* [In Hebrew.] Tel Aviv: Devir, 1968.

Collins, John J. *The Scepter and the Star.* New York: Doubleday, 1995.

Dimant, Devorah. "A Synoptic Comparison of Parallel Sections in 4Q427 7, 4Q491 11 and 4Q471B." *Jewish Quarterly Review* 85 (1994): 157–62.

Eshel, Ester. "4Q Self-Glorification Hymn." In *Qumran Cave 4.XX,* Discoveries in the Judean Desert 29. Oxford: Clarendon Press, 1999, 421–32.

Fleming, Dan. *The Installation of Baal's High Priestess at Emar.* Cambridge MA: Harvard University Press, 1992.

Flusser, David. *Jesus.* Jerusalem: Magnes Press, 1997.

———. *Judaism and the Origins of Christianity.* Jerusalem: Magnes Press, 1998.

———. *Judaism of the Second Temple Period.* Vol. 2, translated by Azan Yadin. Grand Rapids MI: Eerdmans, 2009.

Fredriksen, Paula. *Jesus of Nazareth, King of the Jews.* New York: Knopf, 1999.

Gardiner, Alan H. "The Coronation of King Hamerhab." *Journal of Egyptian Archeology* 39 (1953): 13–31.

Ginsberg, Louis H. *The Israelian Heritage of Judaism.* New York: Jewish Theological Seminary, 1982.

Greenberg, Moshe. "Cities of Asylum." [In Hebrew.] In *Encyclopedia Biblica*, vol. 6, edited by Benjamin Mazar, 383–88. Jerusalem: Bialik Institute, 1971.

Joosten, Jan. "Reflections on the Original Language of the Psalms of Solomon." In *The Psalms of Solomon: Language, History, Theology*, edited by E. Bons and P. Pouchelle, 31–47. Atlanta GA: JBL Press, 2015.

Josephus. *Jewish Antiquities.* Loeb Classical Library. Cambridge MA: Harvard University Press, 1989.

———. *Jewish Wars.* Loeb Classical Library. Cambridge MA: Harvard University Press, 1927.

Kaufmann, Yehezkel. *The History of Israelite Religion.* [In Hebrew.] Jerusalem: Bialik Institute–Devir, 1960.

Klausner, Joseph. *The Messianic Idea in Israel.* Translated by W. F. Stinespring. New York: Macmillan, 1955.

Knohl, Israel. *The Divine Symphony.* Philadelphia: The Jewish Publication Society, 2003.

———. *The Messiah before Jesus.* Berkeley: University of California Press, 2000.

———. *The Sanctuary of Silence.* Minneapolis MN: Fortress Press, 1995.

Kutscher, Yechezkel E. *The Language and the Linguistic Background of the Isaiah Scroll.* [In Hebrew.] Jerusalem: Magnes, 1959.

Loewenstamm, Samuel E. "The Death of Moses." [In Hebrew.] *Tarbiz* 27 (1958): 142–47.

Macintosh, Andrew. *Hosea: A Critical and Exegetical Commentary.* International Critical Commentary. Edinburgh: T & T Clark, 1997.

Martinez, F. G., and E. J. C. Tigchelaar. *The Dead Sea Scrolls: Study Edition.* 2 vols. Leiden: Brill, 1997.

Milgrom, Jacob. *Leviticus 17–22.* Anchor Bible. New York: Doubleday, 2000.

Olyan, Saul. *Violent Rituals of the Hebrew Bible.* New York: Oxford University Press, 2019.

Qimron, Elisha, and John Strugnell. Miqsat Ma'ase Ha-Torah. Discoveries in the Judean Desert 10. Oxford: Clarendon Press, 1994.

Roberts, James J. "Whose Child Is This?" *Harvard Theological Review* 90 (1997): 115–29.

Sanders, E. P. *Jesus and Judaism.* Philadelphia: Fortress Press, 1985.

Schuller, Eileen. "4Q427." In *Qumran Cave 4.XX*, Discoveries in the Judean Desert 29, 77–124. Oxford: Clarendon Press, 1999.

Schweitzer, Albert. *The Quest of the Historical Jesus.* Translated by J. Bowden et al. Minneapolis MN: Fortress Pres, 2001.

Segal, Michael. *The Book of Jubilees.* Leiden: Brill, 2007.

Sievers, Joseph. "Josephus, First Maccabees, Sparta, the Three Haireseis—and Cicero." *Journal for the Study of Judaism* 32 (2001): 241–51.

Talmon, Shemaryahu. "Waiting for the Messiah at Qumran." In *Judaisms and Their Messiahs at the Turn of the Christian Era*, edited by J. Neusner, W. S. Green, and E. S. Freiches. New York: Cambridge University Press, 1987, 11–137.

Talmon, Shemaryahu, and Israel Knohl. "A Calendrical Scroll from Qumran Cave IV." [In Hebrew.] *Tarbiz* 60 (1991): 505–21.

Tigay, Jeffrey H. "Divine Creation of the King in Psalms 2:6." *Eretz Israel* 27 (2003): 246–51.

Weinfeld, Moshe. *Deuteronomy 1–11.* Anchor Bible. New York: Doubleday, 1991.

Wellhausen, Julius. *Die kleinen Propheten übersetzt und erklärt.* [In German.] Berlin: G. Reimer, 1898.

Werman, Cana. *The Book of Jubilees.* [In Hebrew.] Jerusalem: Yad Ben Zvi, 2015.

Williamson, H. G. M. *The Book Called Isaiah.* Oxford: Clarendon, 1994.

Winter, Paul. *On the Trial of Jesus.* Berlin: De Gruyter, 1974.

Wrede, William. *The Messianic Secret.* Translated by J. C. G. Grieg. Cambridge: James Clark, 1971.

Wright, Robert. "Psalms of Solomon." In *The Old Testament Pseudepigrapha*, vol. 2, edited by J. H. Charlesworth, 639–70. New Haven CT: Yale University Press, 1985.

Yarbro-Collins, Adela. "The Charge of Blasphemy in Mark 14.64." *Journal for the Study of the New Testament* 26, no. 4 (2004): 386–91.

————. *Mark: A Commentary.* Hermeneia. Minneapolis MN: Fortress Press, 2007.

Yuditsky, Alex, and Chanan Ariel. "4Q541, Frag. 24 Again." *Dead Sea Discoveries* 23, no. 2 (2016): 221–32.

Zeidel, Moshe. "Parallels between the Books of Isaiah and Psalms." [In Hebrew.] *Sinai* 19 (1956).

Subject Index

Scriptural Index